D1291577

Happier Meals

RETHINKING THE GLOBAL MEAT INDUSTRY

DANIELLE NIERENBERG

Lisa Mastny, *Editor*

WORLDWATCH PAPER 171

September 2005

THE WORLDWATCH INSTITUTE is an independent research organization that works for an environmentally sustainable and socially just society, in which the needs of all people are met without threatening the health of the natural environment or the well-being of future generations. By providing compelling, accessible, and fact-based analysis of critical global issues, Worldwatch informs people around the world about the complex interactions among people, nature, and economies. Worldwatch focuses on the underlying causes of and practical solutions to the world's problems, in order to inspire people to demand new policies, investment patterns, and lifestyle choices.

FINANCIAL SUPPORT for the Institute is provided by ACORE (American Council on Renewable Energy), the Aria Foundation, the Blue Moon Fund, the Fanwood Foundation West, The Ford Foundation, the German Government, Goldman Environmental Prize/Richard & Rhoda Goldman Fund, the W. K. Kellogg Foundation, The Frances Lear Foundation, the Steven C. Leuthold Family Foundation, the Massachusetts Technology Collaborative, the Merck Family Fund, the Norwegian Royal Ministry of Foreign Affairs, The Overbrook Foundation, The David and Lucile Packard Foundation, the V. Kann Rasmussen Foundation, the Rockefeller Brothers Fund, The Shared Earth Foundation, The Shenandoah Foundation, the Tides Foundation, the UN Population Fund, the Wallace Global Fund, the Johanette Wallerstein Foundation, and the Winslow Foundation. The Institute also receives financial support from many individual donors who share our commitment to a more sustainable society.

THE WORLDWATCH PAPERS provide in-depth, quantitative, and qualitative analysis of the major issues affecting prospects for a sustainable society. The Papers are written by members of the Worldwatch Institute research staff or outside specialists and are reviewed by experts unaffiliated with Worldwatch. They have been used as concise and authoritative references by governments, nongovernmental organizations, and educational institutions worldwide. For a partial list of available Worldwatch Papers, go online to www.worldwatch.org/pubs/paper.

Contents

Acknowledgments: I am grateful to the many people who shared their knowledge and criticism for this paper, including Chris Bright, David Brubaker, Christopher Delgado, Diane Farsetta, Bruce Friedrich, Michael Greger, Marlene Halverson, Michael Hansen, Jim Mason, Gaverick Matheny, Harold Mooney, Mark Muller, Michael Pollan, Richard Reynnells, Paul Shapiro, Peter Singer, John Stauber, David Wallinga, and Terry Wollen. I would also like to thank Joyce Nierenberg and Stacy Cordery for their constant encouragement.

At Worldwatch, many colleagues provided thoughtful feedback, including Brian Halweil, Erik Assadourian, Molly Aeck, and Peter Stair. Editor Thomas Prugh helped shape an earlier article, "Factory Farming in the Developing World," which provided the conceptual outline for this paper. Interns Brian Nicholson and Sara Loveland tracked down elusive data and information, while Research Librarian Lori Brown obtained various books and relevant statistics, and provided moral support. Senior Editor Lisa Mastny helped tighten my language and strengthen my argument. Behind the scenes, Art Director Lyle Rosbotham and the Communications team of Darcey Rakestraw and Courtney Berner worked tirelessly to finesse the message I hope to convey.

Danielle Nierenberg is a Research Associate at the Worldwatch Institute, where she studies sustainable agriculture, meat production, animal welfare, food safety, and gender and population issues. Her research has taken her to Asia, Africa, and Latin America, and her work has been published in *World Watch* magazine and the Institute's *State of the World* and *Vital Signs* reports. She has been interviewed for numerous newspapers, including the *International Herald Tribune*, and appeared on national and international radio. Danielle spent two years living in the Dominican Republic as a Peace Corps volunteer and currently helps out at a local farmers market. She holds an M.S. in Agriculture, Food, and Environment from Tufts University and a B.A. in Environmental Policy from Monmouth College.

SUMMARY

O ver the last half century, the human appetite for meat, milk, and eggs has soared in both industrial countries and the developing world. Globalized trade and media, lower meat prices, and urbanization have helped make diets high in animal protein a near-universal aspiration. Meat production has also entered a new era, propelled by cheap feed grains, limited grazing land, readily available antibiotics, and the overall move towards industrializing agriculture.

Today, confined animal feeding operations (CAFOs), or factory farms, account for more than 40 percent of world meat production, up from 30 percent in 1990. Once limited to North America and Europe, they are now the fastest growing form of meat production worldwide. The greatest rise in industrial animal operations is occurring near urban areas of Asia, Africa, and Latin America, where high population densities and weak public health, occupational, and environmental standards are exacerbating the impacts of these farms.

Factory farms were designed to bring animals to market as quickly and cheaply as possible. Yet they invite a host of environmental, animal welfare, and public health problems. Crowded and unhygienic conditions can sicken farm animals and create the perfect environment for the spread of diseases, including outbreaks of avian flu, bovine spongiform encephalopathy (BSE), and foot-and-mouth disease. Factory farms also provide ideal conditions for transmission of illness from livestock to people, and epidemiologists warn of a potentially massive outbreak in congested areas near these operations.

Factory-farmed meat and fish contain an arsenal of unnatural ingredients, including persistent organic pollutants (POPs), polychlorinated biphenyls (PCBs), arsenic, hormones, and other chemicals. Meanwhile the overuse of antibiotics and other antimicrobials in livestock and poultry operations is undermining the toolbox of effective medicines for human use.

The industrialization of meat production has been accompanied by consolidation in the meat industry, so that today a handful of multinational corporations controls most meat production. With this greater concentration, many farmers have lost the connection to their animals and control over their farms. Consumers, too, are increasingly removed from the origins of their food and have little sense of what goes into the hot dogs, hamburgers, milkshakes, and omelets they consume.

Addressing these concerns will require a different approach to the way we raise animals, and a new attitude towards meat as part of the human diet. Ways to reduce the negative consequences of raising and slaughtering large numbers of animals include: educating consumers about the benefits of organic and grass-fed livestock and of vegan and vegetarian diets, supporting small-scale livestock production, encouraging producers to adopt alternative production methods, and improving occupational and welfare standards for both animals and industry workers.

The *Jungle*, Revisited

Since the avian flu outbreak began in southeast Asia in late 2003, public health officials, farmers, veterinarians, government officials, and the media have referred to the disease as a "natural disaster," implying that it was impossible to prevent. But this highly virulent form of avian flu did not just happen. Instead, avian flu, mad cow disease, and other emerging diseases that can spread from animals to humans are symptoms of a larger change taking place in agriculture. Industrial animal production, or factory farming, is like a wave rippling across the world, swallowing up small farms and indigenous animal breeds and concentrating meat production in the hands of a few large companies.

The factory-farm method of raising and slaughtering animals has almost completely taken over Europe and North America. But in much of the developing world, including Brazil, Malaysia, the Philippines, Poland, and Thailand, the tide is just reaching the shore. Everywhere it hits, it is creating ecological and public health disasters, from emerging animal diseases, to air and water pollution, to the loss of livestock genetic resources.

Livestock are an essential part of human existence. They cover a third of the planet's total surface area and use more than two-thirds of its agricultural land, inhabiting nearly every country.[1]* The number of four-footed livestock on Earth at any given moment has increased 38 percent since 1961, from 3.1

---

*Endnotes are grouped by section and begin on page 68.

billion to more than 4.3 billion. India and China boast the largest populations: India's cattle herd exceeds 185 million head, nearly 14 percent of the global total, and China is home to half the world's more than 950 million pigs. The global fowl population, meanwhile, has quadrupled since 1961, from 4.2 billion to 17.8 billion birds.[2]*

Nearly 2 billion people worldwide rely on livestock to support part or all of their daily needs.[3] More than 600 million people are considered small livestock producers, raising goats, cows, cattle, hens, and other animals.[4] And some 200 million people depend on grazing livestock as their only possible source of livelihood.[5] Livestock now supply 30 percent of total human needs for food and agricultural production, converting low-quality biomass, such as corn stalks and other crop residues, into high-quality milk and meat.[6] In the tropics, some 250 million livestock provide draught power as well, helping farmers work 60 percent of the arable land.[7] And livestock fertilize the soil: in developing countries, their manure accounts for about 70 percent of fertility inputs.[8]

Livestock are indispensable for income generation and nutrition in the developing world. They act as living banks, allowing farmers to use them as investments for the future or for quick cash in times of need. Livestock are also an obvious supply of food, providing eggs, milk, meat, blood, and other sources of protein to people all over the world. But the advent of factory farms is breaking the cycle between small farmers, their animals, and the environment.

As livestock numbers grow, our relationship with these animals and their meat is changing. Most of us don't know—or choose not to know—how meat is made because intensive production systems allow us the luxury of not thinking about the implications of factory farming. But meat production has come a long way since the origins of animal domestication. In a very short period, raising livestock has morphed into an industrial endeavor that bears little relation to the landscape or to

---

* In this paper, cattle generally refer to beef-producing bovines and cows refer to dairy cows. Fowl include chickens, ducks, and turkeys.

the natural tendencies of the animals.

Meat once occupied a very different dietary place in the world. A cuisine based on grains and vegetable protein, such as beans, was not some "fringe" diet, but the way most people ate from day to day for much of human history. Beef, pork, chicken, and even eggs were considered luxuries, eaten on special occasions or to enhance the flavor of other foods. Recipes in cookbooks dating from the 1800s and well into the 20th century focus on stretching a small amount of meat over many meals. Instead of having bacon for breakfast, a hamburger for lunch, and steak for dinner, people reserved meat for Sundays or to celebrate holidays. But today, we produce and eat more meat than ever before.

Worldwide, an estimated 258 million tons of meat was produced in 2004, up 2 percent from 2003.[9]* (See Figure 1.) Global meat production has increased more than five-fold since 1950 and more than doubled since the 1970s.[10] Pork accounts for most of this production, followed by chicken and beef.[11] (See Figure 2, page 10.)

Meat consumption is rising fastest not in the United

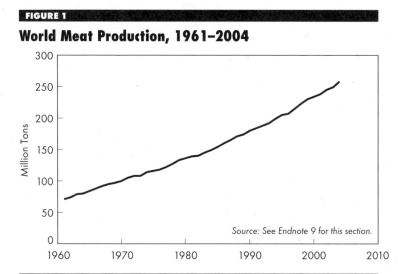

FIGURE 1

World Meat Production, 1961–2004

Source: See Endnote 9 for this section.

* Units of measure throughout this paper are metric unless common usage dictates otherwise.

FIGURE 2

World Meat Production by Source, 2004

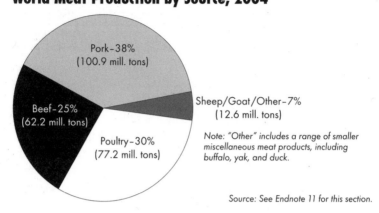

Pork–38%
(100.9 mill. tons)

Beef–25%
(62.2 mill. tons)

Poultry–30%
(77.2 mill. tons)

Sheep/Goat/Other–7%
(12.6 mill. tons)

Note: "Other" includes a range of smaller miscellaneous meat products, including buffalo, yak, and duck.

Source: See Endnote 11 for this section.

States or Europe, but in the developing world, where the average person now consumes nearly 30 kilograms a year.[12] (In industrialized countries, people eat about 80 kilograms of meat a year.) (See Figure 3.) From the early 1970s to the mid-1990s, meat consumption in developing countries grew by 70 million tons, almost triple the rise in industrial countries.[13]

Why the big jump in meat consumption? Christopher Delgado of the Washington, D.C.-based International Food Policy Research Institute (IFPRI) attributes this increase in part to rapid population growth and urbanization, coupled with higher incomes in developing countries. These factors created a "Livestock Revolution" starting in the 1970s, similar to the Green Revolution in cereal production of the 1960s, says Delgado.[14] He notes that traditionally, whenever people have a little extra money to spend on food, they buy more meat. This "nutrition transition," as nutritionists call it, fuels greater demand for chicken, beef, eggs, cheese, and other animal products.[15] In East and Southeast Asia, for example, where income grew 4–8 percent per year between the early 1980s and 1998, population grew 2–3 percent per year, and urbanization grew 4–6 percent per year, meat consumption also increased 4–8 percent per year.[16]

And meat consumption is expected to only rise. IFPRI estimates that by 2020, people in developing countries will consume more than 36 kilograms of meat per person, twice as

FIGURE 3

World Meat Production per Person, 1961–2004

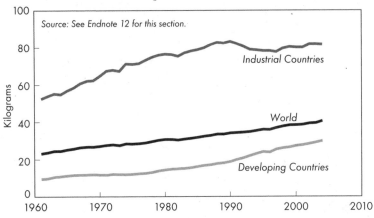

much as in the 1980s.[17] In China, people will consume 73 kilograms a year, a 55 percent increase over 1993, and in Southeast Asia, people are expected to eat 38 percent more meat. Even in Africa, demand for meat in the northern and sub-Saharan regions is expected to nearly double, from 2.4 million tons in 2004 to 5.2 million tons in 2020. People in industrial countries, however, will still consume the most meat—nearly 90 kilograms a year by 2020, the equivalent of a side of beef, 50 chickens, and 1 pig.[18]

As the demand for meat and other animal products increases worldwide, the methods of production are changing. Factory farming is now the fastest growing means of animal production. Although definitions vary by state and by country, factory farms, or confined animal feeding operations (CAFOs) are operations that crowd hundreds of thousands of cows, pigs, chickens, or turkeys together, with little or no access to natural light and fresh air and little opportunity to perform their natural behaviors.* These facilities can produce millions of animals each year.

Industrial systems today generate 74 percent of the

---

* CAFOs refers to both confined animal feeding operations and concentrated animal feeding operations.

world's poultry products, 50 percent of all pork, 43 percent of beef, and 68 percent of eggs.[19] Industrial countries dominate production, but it is in developing nations where livestock producers are rapidly expanding and intensifying their production systems. According to the United Nations Food and Agriculture Organization (FAO), Asia has the fastest developing livestock sector, followed by Latin America and the Caribbean.[20]

The history of industrial meat production began in the early 20th century, when livestock raised on the open ranges of the American West were herded or transported to slaughterhouses and packing mills back east. Upton Sinclair's *The Jungle*, written a century ago when the United States lacked many food safety, environmental, or labor regulations, described in appalling detail the slaughterhouses in Chicago and was a shocking exposé of meat production and the conditions inflicted on both animals and people.[21] Workers were treated much like the animals themselves, forced to labor long hours for very little pay, under dangerous circumstances and with no job security.

The Jungle also predicted the rising influence and power of the meat industry. Today, just four producers control 81 percent of the U.S. beef market.[22] The same is true for chicken and hogs: Tyson Foods, Pilgrim's Pride, and two other companies, for instance, now control 56 percent of the U.S. broiler (meat chicken) industry.[23] Tyson Foods, which touts itself as "the largest provider of protein products on the planet," is the world's biggest meat and poultry company, with more than $26 billion in annual sales and operations in Argentina, Brazil, China, India, Indonesia, Japan, Mexico, the Netherlands, the Philippines, Russia, Spain, the United Kingdom, and Venezuela.[24]* Smithfield Foods, the largest hog producer and pork processor in the world and the fifth-largest beef packer, boasts more than $10 billion in annual sales.[25] More than $1 billion of this is earned internationally from operations in Canada, China, Mexico, and several European countries.[26]

One of the first indications that livestock farming was

---

* Unless otherwise noted, all dollar figures are in U.S. dollars.

COUNTRY STUDY 1

Poland

In 1998, Smithfield Foods president Joseph Luter III told *National Hog Farmer Magazine* he wanted to make Poland the "Iowa of Europe." How? By turning some of the country's richest and most productive land into confined animal feeding operations (CAFOs), similar to those that now dot the landscapes of Iowa and North Carolina in the United States. Smithfield, the world's largest pig producer and pork processor, has its sights set on Poland for several reasons. Land and labor are cheap, and environmental laws are extremely lax. More importantly, Smithfield's Polish operations give it a base in Europe; its local subsidiary, Animex, now operates 29 pig farms in the country, slaughtering some 1.3 million hogs each year.

But this "invasion" of Poland is having disastrous consequences. In Wiekowice, a small town of some 700 people, Animex operates a 12,000-animal pig farm. Unfortunately for the community, the company decided to dispose of the operation's mounting waste near the local elementary school, causing students to vomit and faint. And when Animex moved the disposal site to the other end of its property, near a lake, residents complained that the water had an odd smell, and children who swam in the lake developed eye infections.

Smithfield hasn't brought many new jobs to Poland, either. In fact, the entry of Smithfield and other big industrial hog producers into the Polish market has resulted in overproduction and a drop in hog prices. This has been disastrous for small farmers who no longer have a market for their pigs, but has proven a boon for Smithfield because it lowers the cost of the raw material, without affecting the price of pork in grocery stores.

Some Poles are trying to fight off this invasion. Activists from the U.S.-based Animal Welfare Institute have teamed up with Andrzej Lepper, head of the Polish Farmers' Union, to oppose Smithfield's attempt to take over the Polish hog industry. By illustrating how CAFOs have destroyed many small-scale livestock farms in the United States, they hope to convince Polish farmers and the government to resist corporate agriculture.

Sources: See Endnote 1a, p. 84.

---

changing came in the early 1920s, when Mrs. Cecile Steele, a resident of the Delmarva region of eastern Maryland, mistakenly received a shipment of 500 chicks, instead of the 50 she had ordered to boost the small flock of laying hens she kept for extra income. Rather than returning the chicks, Mrs. Steele decided to capitalize on her error by building a small shed for the birds and raising them indoors—not for their eggs, which she might not have been able to sell, but for their meat. (At that time, chicken meat was not an industry as such but a byproduct of egg-laying flocks.) After her chickens reached two pounds (approx. 1 kilogram), Mrs. Steele sold them for $0.62 a pound, a nice profit during the Depression era and a far better income than she earned from her egg business. News of her success spread quickly, and soon farmers all over Delmarva were imitating Mrs. Steele, positioning the region as the center of U.S. broiler production until just after World War II.[27]

Raising chickens in large numbers meant they could no longer be fed table scraps, and because they were kept indoors, they couldn't hunt and peck for insects. So researchers began developing specialized feeds for broilers. But they encountered a problem: chickens raised indoors didn't get enough sunlight to metabolize calcium properly, leading to rickets and other health concerns. Scientists quickly discovered, however, that putting vitamin D and cod-liver oil into the feed made it possible to raise the birds indoors, in sheds, all year long.[28] They also realized that adding antibiotics to feed caused birds to gain weight more quickly.[29] Eventually, producers had the ability to completely control the chicken's environment, from lighting and temperature to the amount of food.

Farmers everywhere could now raise their chickens indoors, but it took an entrepreneurial truck driver from Arkansas to further challenge the way the birds were produced. In 1936, John Tyson did something no one had tried before: he picked up a load of 500 chickens and drove them 1,000 kilometers north to Chicago, bypassing the local slaughterhouses. That decision, writes Stuart Laidlaw in *Secret Ingredients: The Brave New World of Industrial Farming*, transformed the poultry, pork, and beef industries in not just the United States, but the world.[30]

Tyson proved that chickens could be transported long distances "if the price was right" and broke the tight bond between local farmers and slaughterhouses. He also proved, according to Laidlaw, that slaughterhouses didn't have to buy the birds closest to them to get the cheapest price.[31] Tyson didn't stop at transporting chickens either. By buying up feed plants, starting hatcheries, contracting with producers, and building processing plants, he eventually created a system of vertical integration whereby Tyson Foods owns each of its millions of chickens from before they hatch to the day they're slaughtered. These technological changes made it easier to standardize chicken production and propelled the shift toward factory farming.

Tyson wasn't the only one interested in boosting chicken production. During World War II, nationwide rationing of red meat led to increased consumer demand for chicken in the United States. To fulfill the promise of "a chicken in every pot," retailers became interested in using genetics to improve poultry production, specifically breeding birds for their meat qualities. Breeders began to develop new strains of chicken that could produce a meaty, large-breasted carcass at low feed cost—in other words, a chicken that could eat less and weigh more.[32] Before 1946, it took an average of 112 days to produce a 1.7-kilogram broiler, with inputs of 13.3–22 kilograms of feed for every kilogram of weight gained.[33] Today, broilers eat less than half the feed and reach 2 kilograms in about one-third the time.[34]

But the picture isn't pretty. Factory-farmed laying hens look very different from the ones Cecile Steele and other farmers' wives raised in the 1920s. They are crammed together in small wire cages where they can't stand upright, spread their wings, or perform any of their natural behaviors. The life of a broiler isn't much happier, packed with thousands of other birds in a long shed with little leg or wing room.[35] (See Sidebar 1, page 16.)

Starting in the early 1960s, pigs and cows, too, began being raised on factory farms. Like the poultry industry, the pig industry is now almost completely vertically integrated in the United States. Artificially inseminated sows (female pigs) are kept in gestation crates that prevent them from turning around or performing most of their natural behaviors. Dairy cows,

SIDEBAR 1

The Life of a Chicken

Most chickens follow one of two paths: they are raised to lay eggs (layers) or only for their meat (broilers). They begin their journey along the industrial food chain in breeding farms owned by Tyson Foods, Pilgrim's Pride, or some other agribusiness company. There, eggs are kept warm by carefully controlled incubators. Breeders make sure chicks all hatch at close to the same time by artificially inseminating the mother hens. After hatching, chicks destined to be layers come into contact with humans for the first, and often the only, time. Workers sex the chicks when they are one day old, tossing the males into large bins where they are later ground up (sometimes still alive) for use as fertilizer or animal feed.

Females are put on an assembly line and painfully debeaked with hot blades. After 18–20 weeks, the chicks (along with feed and other inputs) are shipped to contract growers. The layers are housed in 18-by-110 meter (60-by-360-foot) barns (as are the broilers)—about half the size of a football field. Each barn can hold more than 90,000 chickens, and with the help of high-tech equipment, one farmer can usually manage an entire barn with little help.

Once on the farm, each laying hen is put into a wire battery cage with as many as nine other birds. Hens are tricked into laying more eggs by round-the-clock artificial lighting. Their cages, stacked one on top of the other and covered in dripping feces, allow for little movement. The hens are easily startled because they rarely have any human contact. Usually the only birds that producers have to touch are those that have somehow escaped from a cage or have died from stress.

Not surprisingly, chickens kept in these conditions are more susceptible to disease and tend to die much earlier than traditionally raised chickens. In fact, after a year or so most hens are so worn out that their egg production declines. Broiler chickens have an even shorter lifespan. Although they are not kept in individual cages, broilers are packed tightly into sheds with little leg or wing room—each bird is given about 23 by 23 centimeters (9 by 9 inches) of floor space. They are not exposed to outside light or fresh air, and they have unnaturally long days because the windowless sheds are lit for up to 23 hours a day.

Each day these chickens eat about 70–100 grams of specially designed feed, which may contain antibiotics or growth promoters. Although chickens are efficient at converting grain into protein, their living conditions make them very susceptible to respiratory diseases. So producers have a long history of adding to the feed antibiotics much like those used to treat human disease. (A study in 2002 found that 37 percent of the broilers found in major grocery stores are contaminated with antibiotic-resistant pathogens.) When they weigh about 2 kilograms, broilers are rounded up by workers known as catchers, stuffed into cages, and taken to processing plants. Workers sort, cut, and weigh the chickens for distribution to grocery stores and restaurants. Some packages carry warnings to consumers to cook chicken completely to prevent the meat, often contaminated with feces, from spreading food-borne illnesses.

But not all farmers are raising chickens in factories. According to the U.N. Food and Agriculture Organization (FAO), backyard and free-range chickens account for as much as 70 percent of both egg and meat production in some of the poorest countries. Farmers can use chickens, says Robyn Alders of FAO, as a "kind of credit card, instantly available for sale or barter in societies where cash is not abundant." They are also an important source of pest control and fertilizer. Projects in Bangladesh and South Africa are improving poultry health, providing income for members of poor communities, and giving native chicken breeds—which are already adapted to heat and low-input conditions—a chance to survive.

Sources: See Endnote 35 for this section.

meanwhile, live their short lives in either indoor stalls or drylots, outdoor enclosures that can hold thousands of animals, typically with little or no grass, bedding, or protection from the weather. In addition to their feed, they receive injections of recombinant growth hormone (rBGH), a genetically engineered hormone that forces them to produce more milk.[36] Ironically, as livestock production increases in the U.S., the number of individual farms raising these animals is on the decline. In 1950, there were approximately 2 million pig farms nationwide, producing nearly 80 million pigs. Today, there are only 73,600 operations, raising more than 100 million pigs per year.[37] Government subsidies and cheap prices for corn have pushed much of this concentration, giving large-scale livestock farmers an advantage over their smaller-sized counterparts.

The influence of these companies on agriculture doesn't stop at the U.S. border, either. If *The Jungle* were written today, it would not be set in the American Midwest. As environmental and labor regulations in the European Union and the United States become stronger and more prohibitive, large agribusinesses are moving their animal production operations overseas, primarily to countries with less stringent enforcement. From China and Brazil to India and the former Soviet Union, meat is now a globalized product, controlled by a handful of multinational companies.

But the problems Sinclair pointed to a century ago, including hazardous working conditions, unsanitary processing methods, and environmental contamination, still exist. Many have worsened. The billions of tons of manure that pollute our water and air are effectively creating mini "agricultural Chernobyls," with the potential for even more widespread destruction. Meanwhile, the economic landscape of confined animal operations subjugates workers, local communities, and independent farmers.

The Disassembly Line

It's easy to forget how meat is made. The neatly wrapped packages at the supermarket give little indication of how the animals that end up on our dinner tables, or the people who raised and butchered them, were treated. The labels on the front don't show hens crippled and deformed from living in wired cages, mother pigs crammed into gestation crates, or cattle standing in seas of manure in feedlots.

Nor do they offer a glimpse of the lost limbs of meat processors or the scarred hands of chicken handlers. "Killing and cutting up the animals we eat has always been bloody, hard, and dangerous work," notes a January 2005 report by Human Rights Watch. "Meatpacking plants at the turn of the twentieth century were more than sweatshops. They were blood shops, and not only for animal slaughter. The industry operated with low wages, long hours, brutal treatment, and sometimes deadly exploitation of mostly immigrant workers. Meatpacking companies had equal contempt for public health."[1]

Although conditions improved from the 1930s to the 1970s (thanks to the hard work of public health advocates and labor unions), more recent changes in the American meat industry have once again created environments similar to those described in *The Jungle* a century ago. In the 1980s, meat plants moved from Chicago and other urban centers to rural areas, closer to the factory farms that supplied them. And with these new locations, says Human Rights Watch, processors like the Iowa Beef Processors (IBP) changed the way meat is cut up and distributed. IBP and its "copycat producers" in the industry automated the process, reducing every stage to the same repetitive cutting motions in what is commonly referred to as the "disassembly line."[2]

Because margins in the industry are so narrow, producers try to squeeze out profit wherever they can. They speed up slaughtering and cutting lines and often fail to provide the proper equipment. They force their employees to work in filthy, cold, and slippery environments and require them to put in long days, sometimes more than 12 hours at a time. All of these conditions make meatpacking one of the most dangerous jobs in America. Injury rates for workers along the disassembly line—from the knockers who literally knock pigs or cows unconscious to the navel boners and splitters who slice and carve the meat that eventually appears on the dinner plate—are three times higher than in a typical American factory. Every year, one in three meatpacking workers suffers an injury on the job. But because many of these workers are undocumented immigrants or struggle at the very bottom of the economic ladder, many don't report their injuries, making the actual number far higher.[3]

Chicken catchers, as they are called, have the unfortunate job of literally picking up by hand the thousands of broiler chickens that inhabit factory farms. They go in at night, grab five or six chickens at a time per hand, and stuff them into wire cages as fast as they can. As at meatpacking plants, many U.S. chicken catchers are Mexican or African-American. They are paid not by the hour, but by how many birds they catch each night, sharing a meager $2 for every 1,000 chickens caught and making only about $100 each for an eight-hour shift.[4] The job is dangerous, and workers are often scarred by beaks and claws.

Such injuries and health concerns aren't confined to the United States. At the largest government-owned slaughtering plant in the Philippines, located in Manila, workers stun, bludgeon, and slaughter animals at a breakneck pace.[5] They wear little protective gear as they slide on floors slippery with blood, making it hard to stun animals on the first or even second try or to butcher meat without injuring themselves. Workers are also poorly trained in how to humanely stun and slaughter animals—by using stun guns, for instance—which can further increase injury rates as well as inhumane treatment of animals. On-the-job injuries and illnesses are particularly devastating in developing countries because most workers lack insurance as well as workers' compensation benefits.

Meat workers also suffer, not surprisingly, from mental health problems related to the nature of their work. Turnover rates in the industry are high not only because of the physical injuries they risk, but because of the mental anguish many of them endure, slaughtering and processing animals every day.[6]

Mental and physical injuries aren't restricted to workers, of course; the billions of animals raised in these farms experience physical and behavioral problems as well. Confinement of veal calves may be one of the most well-known and egregious examples of cruelty in the livestock industry. Taken from their mothers just days after birth, the calves are confined in tiny crates that prevent them from moving more than a few steps. Calves thrive on interaction, but these crates prevent them from being with other animals. For the entire 16 weeks of their lives, they are alone, unable to stretch or lie down comfortably or groom themselves. Fed from buckets, the calves also cannot suckle normally, resulting in neurotic behaviors such as sucking and chewing their crates. A rich diet of liquid formula keeps their meat very pale and tender, the kind most restaurants prefer, although there seems to be no taste difference between this pale veal and the pinker veal of calves fed small amounts of solid food.[7]

Female pigs, too, live most of their lives in crates roughly 60 centimeters wide by 2 meters long (2 feet by 7 feet), unable to stand or turn around. After giving birth, the sow's piglets are weaned as early as three weeks of age. They are then crowded into barren cages devoid of bedding material, denying them the ability to root around. Not surprisingly, these stressful conditions provoke abnormal or aggressive behavior, such as tail biting. As a result, producers simply dock pigs' tails or cut their eye teeth, without anesthesia. When the piglets reach about 23 kilograms (50 pounds) they are sent to "finishing" barns where they spend four months reaching their ideal slaughter weight of 113 kilograms (250 pounds). These facilities are massive, often spreading out over hundreds of acres and housing thousands of pigs at a time.[8]

Fish, too, are beginning to be raised in more intensive, industrial style conditions. These "factory farms of the sea" can have the same sort of problems as those on land.[9] (See Sidebar 2, page 22.)

While the living conditions of these animals are bad enough, they often get worse during the final hours at the slaughterhouse. People for the Ethical Treatment of Animals (PETA), one of the most well-known animal welfare groups, has documented stunning instances of abuse inside factory farms in the United States. At a KFC-restaurant supplier in West Virginia, workers were filmed stomping on birds, throwing chickens against walls, and tearing them apart, all while the birds were fully conscious. "Workers are treated badly by a farmed animal industry that is consolidating the cutting labor costs and benefits to the lowest levels possible, so we've found that workers often take their frustration out on animals," says PETA's director of vegan campaigns, Bruce Friedrich.[10]

Not surprisingly, slaughtering facilities stress animals in other ways. Cattle and cows, for example, do not like to walk up or down steep inclines, but many facilities force animals up ramps. Livestock often watch one another being slaughtered, or can see and smell blood.

These industrial-style methods aren't good for the bottom line or for the quality of the finished product either. Research indicates that when animals experience stress prior to slaugh-

SIDEBAR 2

Factory Farms of the Sea

The global appetite for fish has doubled over the last thirty years. But because of depletion of wild stocks, virtually all the growth in the catch today comes not from the ocean, but from fish raised on farms, or aquaculture. The aquaculture harvest has doubled in just the last decade, to nearly 40 million tons, and now accounts for 30 percent of the total fish harvest. By 2020, aquaculture could produce nearly half of all fish harvested.

As the demand for fish skyrockets, producers are adopting more intensive, industrial-style methods, which can cause the same sorts of problems as those on land. Farmed salmon, for example, spend the 2–3 years of their lives crammed into pens, where they are fed high-protein fish meal. This practice of giving farmed fish the ground-up bits of other marine species results in a net loss to world fish production: according to a study in *Nature*, for the ten types of fish most commonly farmed, an average of 1.9 kilograms of wild fish is required for every kilogram of farmed fish. The United States is now proposing the next phase of fish farming: open-ocean aquaculture, or the construction of penned farms for large carnivorous fish fattened with fish meal, located more than 300 kilometers offshore.

As with livestock, farmed fish often contain a range of unexpected ingredients. They require massive doses of antibiotics and pesticides to prevent diseases that result from overcrowding, including sea lice, a parasite that can spread quickly in crowded pens. Farmed salmon also have higher levels of polychlorinated biphenyls (PCBs) and other toxins than wild-caught fish. A 2004 study in *Science* found that farmed salmon had dioxin levels 11 times higher than in wild-caught salmon, while PCB levels averaged 36.6 parts per billion (ppb), versus only 4.75 ppb for the wild fish. Meanwhile, producers inject farmed salmon with artificial food coloring to turn their flesh the more desirable pink of wild salmon.

The effects of fish farms can spill into surrounding waters and communities. Effluent from ponds and pens, including fertilizer, undigested feed, and fish waste, is often released directly into streams and rivers, causing eutrophication and damaging soil and water quality. Ocean-based fish farms can pollute the ocean floor, destroying habitat for bottom-dwelling species. And shrimp farming along coasts has caused the destruction of thousands of hectares of valuable mangrove forests.

Farmed fish can escape from pens as well, interbreeding with wild species and competing for their food. Because farmed fish are bred for

specific traits, interbreeding could lead to the loss of genetic adapta-
tions that have allowed wild fish to survive. Transgenic fish could be particularly dangerous to wild species: because these modified fish are
usually bigger, they are more efficient at spreading their DNA, although
their offspring are less likely to survive into adulthood.

Sources: See Endnote 9 for this section.

ter, they use up the glycogen in their muscles, decreasing levels of lactic acid that make meat tender and give it good color.
Rough handling at feedlots and slaughterhouses can also
bruise animals, lowering meat quality and resulting in an estimated loss of $60–$70 per head.[11]

Appetite for Destruction

Even the most cursory examination of modern meat production would indicate serious environmental and public health problems as well, ranging from disease and antibiotic
resistance to ecosystem degradation and unhealthy diets. As
meat-eating becomes a global aspiration (sometimes legitimate,
sometimes in excess), and as the world's livestock herds soar
to unprecedented levels, the scale and severity of this fallout
will only grow.

Consider what goes into producing meat and other animal products.[1] (See Figure 4, page 24.) One of the biggest and
fastest growing inputs is grain, primarily cheap corn and soybeans, now used as feed in livestock operations around the
world. In the United States, 70 percent of the corn harvest is
fed to livestock.[2] And worldwide, nearly 80 percent of all soybeans are used for animal feed.[3]

Why are today's livestock fed so much grain? The answer
is simple: it makes them gain weight, fast. Steers used to live
at least 4–5 years before being slaughtered. Today, beef calves
can grow from 36 kilograms to 544 kilograms in just 14 months
on a diet of corn, soybeans, antibiotics, and hormones.[4]

Corn, in particular, provides the fuel for building "fast

FIGURE 4

The Ins and Outs of Meat Production

INPUTS

Feed
• A calorie of beef, pork, or poultry needs 11–17 calories of feed.
• 80 percent of soybean harvest is eaten by animals, not people.
• Feed containing meat and bone meal can cause mad cow disease, which has affected thousands of cattle in industrial countries.

Water
• Producing 8 ounces of beef can require up to 25,000 liters of water.

Additives
• Cows, pigs, and chickens get 70 percent of all antimicrobial drugs in the United States.

Fossil Fuels
• A calorie of beef takes 33 percent more fossil-fuel energy to produce than a calorie of energy from potatoes would.

OUTPUTS

Manure
• Manure from intensive pig operations stored in lagoons can leak into groundwater or pollute nearby surface water.

Methane
• Belching, flatulent livestock emit 16 percent of the world's annual production of methane, a powerful greenhouse gas.

Disease
• Eating animal products high in saturated fat and cholesterol is linked to cancer, heart disease, other chronic illnesses.
• Factory farm conditions can spread *E. coli*, *Salmonella*, and other food-borne pathogens.
• Creutzfeldt-Jakob disease, the human variant of mad cow disease, has killed at least 150 people.

Sources: See Endnote 12 for this section.

food nations." According to agriculture and food writer Michael Pollan, "a [McDonald's] Chicken McNugget is corn upon corn upon corn, beginning with corn-fed chicken all the way through the obscure food additives and the corn starch that holds it together. All the meat at McDonald's is really corn. Chickens have become machines for converting two pounds of corn into one pound of chicken. The beef, too, is from cattle fed corn on feedlots." Without the cheap, abundant supplies of corn and soybeans in the United States, Pollan notes, factory farming could never have occurred.[5]

But eating corn doesn't come naturally to cows. Cattle are ruminants, meaning they digest grasses and crop residues easily. Their standard feedlot ration, in contrast, is a mixture of high-protein corn, soybeans, and other ingredients that are much harder to stomach. Cattle (and other animals) on this diet gain weight quickly, however, and fatter livestock bring a higher market price.[6]

Although many consumers have come to expect the taste, texture, and appearance of industrial meat, soft and marbled with fat, this grain-fed product has hidden costs for both animals and people. First, cows tend to suffer from bloating, acidosis, liver abscesses, gas, and other symptoms of this rich diet. In fact, when they're eating grass calves don't need any medication or antimicrobial drugs, but as soon as they begin a grain diet, they start to get sick. The shift so disturbs the animal's digestive system that it can die if this transition is not carefully managed.[7]

Meanwhile, the standard diet in factory farms has been linked to the spread of food-borne pathogens, such as *Escherichia coli* 0157:H7 (*E. coli*), which can contaminate meat or even vegetables if the raw manure is used as fertilizer. Whereas a grass diet eliminates this harmful microbe, the grain diet encourages its growth in a cow's stomach.[8]

There's also something fishy about what livestock are being fed. A growing share of the global fish harvest is now ground up and mixed into the grain fed to livestock. About a third of the total marine fish catch is utilized for fish meal, two-thirds of which goes to chickens, pigs, and other animals.[9] This is despite the fact that fisheries all over the world are being fished out, threatening the lives and livelihoods of millions of people.

But livestock aren't just eating more seafood—they're also eating each other. Although regulations in the United Kingdom prohibit feeding meat and bone meal to cattle to prevent bovine spongiform encephalopathy (BSE, or mad cow disease), livestock elsewhere are still being fed the ground-up bits and pieces of other animals. In the United States, for example, it is still legal to feed cattle beef tallow. Producers also give cattle cow's blood, chicken, chicken manure, feather meal, pigs, and even sawdust.[10]* The European Union, on the other hand, has banned feeding pigs, chickens, and cattle feed containing any animal protein.[11] Mexican feed makers, following the lead of American companies, grind up dead chickens to feed back to other birds.[12]

Industrial livestock production can be extremely resource intensive as well. Drop for drop, animal production is one the biggest consumers of water worldwide. Grain-fed beef is several times more water consumptive than most other foods: producing just 0.2 kilograms (8 ounces) of beef can use 25,000 liters of water.[13] In contrast, producing enough flour in developing countries to make a loaf of bread requires just 550 liters of water.[14]

The meat-consumption choices of less-developed nations over the coming decades will have a significant effect on the world's water resources, according to a 2004 report by the United Nations Commission on Sustainable Development.[15] If this demand is directed toward grain-fed or feedlot beef production, the additional water requirements would be on the order of 1,500 cubic kilometers, equivalent to the annual flow of India's Ganges River. On the other hand, if preferences were for pasture- or grass-raised chickens, pigs, and cattle, water demand would be less drastic. In general, diets in the most populated and water-stressed regions of the world are moving towards more meat, not less. As a result, land and water are being diverted away from the production of foods that require less water and are also essential for nutritional security, such as beans and high-protein grains.[16]

The other end of the production process, slaughtering and processing animals, can be equally water intensive. The United Nations Environment Programme estimates that 2,000-15,000 liters of water are used per live-weight ton of slaughtered animal in the United States; most of that water, an estimated 44-60 percent is used in the slaughter, evisceration, and boning

---

* In 1997, the U.S. Food and Drug Administration adopted a ban on feeding ruminants to ruminants, but loopholes in the ruling still allow cattle to be fed a wide range of animal products.

areas of abattoirs.[17]* One slaughterhouse in Hong Kong gen-
erates 5 million liters of waste water per day.[18]

Oil, too, is a necessary ingredient of modern meat production. Each stage of production, from growing feed to transporting and processing animals, is highly energy intensive.
Producing one calorie of beef takes 33 percent more fossil
fuel energy than producing a calorie of potatoes.[19] CAFOs
themselves require huge amounts of energy for heating, cool-
ing, and lighting. Contract farmers bear most of these costs but
are paid the same amount by the companies they work for,
regardless of fluctuations in energy prices.

The inefficient inputs to factory farms are mirrored by
inefficient outputs. On June 22, 1995, the wall of an artificial
waste lagoon gave way at a pig operation in the U.S. state of
North Carolina, spilling some 95 million liters of putrefying
urine and feces across several fields, over a road, and into the
New River.[20] Millions of fish and other aquatic organisms
died in what has become one of the worst incidents of water
pollution in the state's history. Unfortunately, it wasn't an isolated event. A few weeks after the New River spill, 34 million
liters of poultry waste flowed down a North Carolina creek into
the Northeast Cape Fear River. That August, another 3.8 million liters of pig waste trickled through a network of tidal
creeks into the Cape Fear Estuary.[21]

But the worst was yet to come. Strong hurricanes in 1998
and 1999 brought a series of massive floods to the North Carolina seaboard, drowning thousands of pigs trapped in factory
farms and unleashing untold millions of liters of lagoon
waste.[22] North Carolina is a perfect example of what can happen when hog production increases too quickly. In 1987, the
state produced a mere 2.6 million hogs per year. Today, it
produces 10 million (more than the number of state residents), generating some 19 million tons of pig waste annually.[23]

Like human sewage, CAFO waste is extremely high in
nitrogen, much of which comes from animal feed—or rather,

---

* According to UNEP, rates of water consumption can vary considerably
depending on the scale of the plant, the age and type of processing, the level
of automation, and cleaning practices.

COUNTRY STUDY 2

Mexico

Take a tour through Eugenio Salinas Morales' office at the Mexican Meat Consortium in Mexico City and you'll get an idea of the growing strength of the meat industry there. Dozens of posters of domestic brand-name meats and meat products line the walls in glass frames, and it's Morales's job to keep them all competitive in the global marketplace. One way Mexico is doing that is by encouraging farmers and agribusiness companies to scale-up their production.

Local producers of eggs, poultry, beef, and milk are disappearing rapidly in Mexico, being replaced by large companies that engage smaller farmers as contract growers. Today, about half of the country's pork production occurs on factory farms and 95 percent of egg production is from industrial systems. Chicken farming is almost entirely vertically integrated, with each company owning nearly every stage of production, from "egg to plate." Because of this integration, says Sergio Gomez, a researcher with Mexico's National Center for the Investigation of Animal Physiology (INIFAP), the big producers act as a "mafia," making it difficult for smaller, independent farmers to find slaughterhouses and processing facilities for their meat.

Two of Mexico's largest chicken companies are Industrías Bachoco, a local company, and Pilgrim's Pride, based in the United States. Smaller companies include Nutribaq, the largest producer of chicken feed in the state of Querétaro and the owner of several large poultry farms. Following the lead of Pilgrim's and other American companies, Nutribaq has adopted a "cost-effective" way to recycle chickens that die of stress before reaching maturity. A Nutribaq truck simply makes the rounds of each farm, collecting dead chickens and bringing them to the company's feed factories, where they are pulverized and later fed back to live chickens in Nutribaq feed.

INIFAP, in conjunction with the U.N. Food and Agriculture Organization (FAO), is currently conducting studies to identify the environmental risks of factory farming in northern Mexico. The town of La Piedad has the highest concentration of big factory farms, mostly of chickens, anywhere in the country. And in nearby Tepatitlan, more than 25 million hens are being raised in factory farms. Of particular concern are the high levels of nitrogen and phosphorous from chicken manure in the surface and groundwater. According to INIFAP, all farms in this area are releasing contaminants in quantities that exceed the recommended levels. As industrial agriculture expands in the region, INIFAP and FAO plan to continue working on ways to control the pollution.

While this joint effort is a step forward in making Mexico's livestock production more environmentally sound, the country has made less progress
in promoting animal welfare. Few big producers have adopted humane
methods of raising animals, and no legislation exists to protect farm animals from abuse. Even at an INFIAP project site in Querétaro, pigs are
raised intensively in stalls with concrete floors, their tails docked and with
little or no bedding.

Sources: See Endnote 2a, p. 84.

---

from the fertilizer used to grow it. In a sense, factory farms owe
their existence to the advent of chemical fertilizer, which has
allowed for the uncoupling of livestock and crops. Natural
manure, when used to fertilize crops, enriches the soil and is
a key input to a healthy farm. But when farmers get their fertilizer from a bag, they don't need to use manure. And just as
readily as fertilizer can be shipped to corn growers, the feed corn
it nourishes can be shipped to factory farms. In each case, the
basic input is no longer produced by the landscape in which
it is used, so the local ecology no longer effectively limits the
intensity of production. As the environmental costs mount,
however, this fractured system is likely to be untenable over
the long term.[24]

Even if CAFO operators wanted to use the manure produced at their facilities, there is usually not enough land
nearby to handle it. In the United States, livestock produce more
than 600 million tons of waste annually on factory farms.[25] In
a typical industrial pig operation, each of the 20,000 or so sows
will produce about 20 piglets over the course of a year. Just one
sow and her piglets will excrete some 1.9 tons of manure
annually, enough to fill the back of a standard pick-up truck.[26]

The logistics of managing this waste are formidable.
Since lagoon space is limited, CAFOs require huge amounts of
"spreadable acreage," cropland on nearby farms where manure
can be spread, sprayed, or injected. But if you're trying to do
a conscientious job of it, finding adequate spreadable acreage
is a difficult task; a 20,000-animal operation would need about
30,000 spreadable hectares.[27] Inevitably, given the size of most
factory farms, this ideal is rarely attained. Either too much

manure is spread on the fields, contributing more nitrogen than the crops can handle, or worse, it is spread at the wrong time, when a crop cannot effectively take up the nutrients. In other instances, the manure is spread on fields of nitrogen-fixing crops like soybeans and alfalfa, which require little or no additional fertilizer. Only about half of all livestock waste is effectively fed into the crop cycle.[28] Much of the remainder ends up polluting the air, water, and soil itself.

Nitrate from manure can seep into groundwater, creating serious public health risks. High nitrate levels in wells near feedlot operations in the United States have been linked to greater risk of miscarriage.[29] In extreme cases, nitrate contamination can cause methemoglobinemia, or "blue-baby syndrome," a form of infant poisoning in which the blood's ability to transport oxygen is greatly reduced, sometimes to the point of death. High levels of nitrate have also been linked to cancer.[30]

In the 1990s, as many as one-third of all wells in the chicken-producing region along Maryland's lower Eastern Shore and southern Delaware exceeded the U.S. Environmental Protection Agency's (EPA's) safe drinking water standards for nitrate, according to a study by the U.S. Geological Survey. The region's farms raise more than 600 million birds a year and produce some 750,000 tons of manure, more than a city of 4 million people. The EPA estimates that poultry operations in Maryland, Delaware, and Virginia send more than three times as much phosphorous into the Chesapeake Bay as municipal sewage treatment plants.[31] These operations may be partly to blame for outbreaks of *pfisteria pescicida*, a toxic algae that can kill fish and sicken people, in the Bay in the late 1990s. *Pfisteria* and other algaes thrive in nitrogen- and phosphorous- rich water, choking out other life.

But as anyone who lives near a CAFO can tell you, water contamination is hardly the most noticeable environmental effect. If raw manure is exposed to the air, a large percentage of the nitrogen in it can escape as gaseous ammonia (NH_3), resulting in an olfactory experience that's difficult to forget.[32] Scientists suspect that exposure to manure can also lead to public health problems including depression, anxiety, and fatigue.[33]

Pig lagoons, for example, release hydrogen sulfide, causing headaches and respiratory ailments among farm workers and nearby residents.[34]

The same story is being played out around the world. Foremost Farms, north of Manila in the Philippines, is one of the largest "piggeries" in Asia, producing an estimated 100,000 animals annually. High walls prevent people in the community from seeing what goes on inside, but they do get a whiff of the waste. Not only can neighbors smell the manure created by the 20,000 hogs kept at Foremost and the 10,000 hogs kept at nearby Holly Farms, but their water supply has been polluted by it. Residents have complained of skin rashes, infections, and other health problems. But instead of keeping the water clean and installing effective waste treatment, the farms are just digging deeper wells and granting free access to them. Many in the community are reluctant to complain because they fear losing their water supply. Even the mayor of Bulacan, the nearby village, has said "we give these farms leeway as much as possible because they provide so much economically."[35]

Excess manure is causing nutrient imbalances near rapidly expanding operations in China, Thailand, and Vietnam as well. According to a recent study by Pierre Gerber with the U.N. Food and Agriculture Organization, livestock production in the region is growing faster than crop production, forcing "a divorce" between the two systems. "While farmers with five pigs can have a well managed, well developed, closed-loop recycling system where they use manure to fertilize their crops, that is well controlled from a public health point-of-view, farmers with 500 or more pigs can no longer follow these ancient practices," Gerber notes. And because the manure from industrial operations is different than the manure produced on traditional farms, there are questions of how to use and dispose of it without harming the environment or human health.[36]

Because it's a waste product, manure can contain significant amounts of bacteria, in addition to other undigested residues. Citizens of Walkerton, Ontario, learned that bacteria from cattle waste can show up where they least expect it—out of the water taps in their homes. In the spring of 2000, more than 1,000 residents fell sick and four people died from *E. coli* after the municipal water system became contaminated with runoff from a nearby feedlot.[37] Manure can also contain antibiotics, hormones, and heavy metals. According to a recent study, 25–75 percent of the antimicrobials given to livestock may pass through undigested, resulting in traces of these drugs as well as antibiotic-resistant bacteria in the animals' waste.[38] Humans can be exposed to these drugs on a daily basis, reducing the efficacy of the medicines when people really need them. (See "Spreading Disease," below.)

Meanwhile, hormones used to increase milk and meat production can end up in the water and soil, disrupting the endocrine systems of fish and other wildlife. In one study, researchers found that fish exposed to feedlot effluent had significant damage to their reproductive systems: male fish experienced demasculinization, with decreased testis size, and female fish had lower estrogen levels.[39] Hormone-rich runoff from fields fertilized with manure can also threaten human health. Researchers at Tufts University report that exposure to endocrine-disrupting hormones can increase the risks of breast and ovarian cancer in women and testicular cancer in men, and can lower male sperm quality and count.[40]

But it's not just our air and water that are being contaminated. Surprisingly, animal waste can also seep into oil wells, threatening oil supplies. A case filed in Illinois in 2004 by Test Drilling Service Company against a pig farm alleges that liquid waste leaking from the farm's lagoons contaminated nearby wells, making the oil unsellable.[41]

Spreading Disease

I n addition to polluting the environment and endangering public health, factory farming is threatening the diversity of the world's livestock herds, with wider implications for human and animal survival.[1] As people eat more meat, eggs, milk, and other animal products, farmers are forced to abandon local breeds in favor of a limited number of high-producing livestock. While pastoralists and small livestock breeders have traditionally bred their animals to resist certain diseases or to survive in hot climates, commercial breeders select for traits that will earn them the most money, including the ability of animals to gain weight quickly, produce more milk, or, in the case of poultry, to have meatier breasts and more white meat. These commercial breeds are rarely allowed to mate naturally; instead, producers artificially inseminate animals and even import sperm to maintain complete control over their flocks and herds.

Within the last century, 1,000 breeds—about 15 percent of the world's cattle and poultry varieties—have disappeared, according to the U.N. Food and Agriculture Organization (FAO).[2] About 300 of these losses occurred in just the past 15 years, and many more breeds are in danger of extinction.[3] (See Table 1, page 34.) The problem has been greatest in industrial countries, where factory farming is most intense; in Europe, more than half of all breeds of domestic animals that existed a century ago have disappeared, and 43 percent of remaining breeds are endangered.[4] But as developing countries rise up the protein ladder, the genetic stock of their livestock is also eroding as higher-producing industrial breeds crowd out indigenous varieties.[5]

This creeping homogeneity doesn't just threaten the genetic variability of species, it handicaps the ability of farmers everywhere to respond to changes in climate, pests, and especially disease. Because meat is a globalized product, with meat and live cattle being shipped across borders and across oceans, diseases like avian flu, bovine spongiform encephalopathy (BSE), and foot-and-mouth can become global phenomena. Many of these ailments were first discovered in animals, but can eventually spread to humans.[6] (See Table 2, page 35.) The overuse of antimicrobials for livestock, meanwhile, is undermining our toolbox of human medicines.

Factory farms provide the perfect conditions for disease to spread from livestock to people, and epidemiologists are

TABLE 1

Selected Food Animal Breeds in Danger of Disappearing

Breed	Importance	Status
Lulu cattle	Native to Nepal, the Lulu are well adapted to extreme environments and are highly disease-resistant. They require few inputs and are extremely productive, yielding up to two liters of milk a day.	Endangered as a result of rampant crossbreeding because indigenous breeds are seen as inferior to exotic breeds.
South China pig	A hardy breed, it is adapted to poor feed and highly resistant to heat and direct solar radiation. It is also immune to kidney worm and liver fluke, unlike foreign pig breeds.	Because of the intensification of factory farming in Malaysia, there are only about 400 of these pigs left.
Mukhatat chicken	Native to Iraq, it can be raised in harsh environments with little nutritional requirements.	Fewer than 600 individuals remain.
Criolla Mora sheep	A Colombian sheep that can be traced back to 1548, Criolla Mora are used for meat and wool and are resistant to endoparasite infestation.	Scientists are uncertain how many remain—anywhere from 100 to 1,000 live in the Colombian highlands.
Warsaw grouper	A resident of the southwest Atlantic and popular for its white, flaky meat, the grouper can reach over 300 pounds.	Are territorial and never leave their immediate habitat, making them an easy catch. Face "extremely high risk" of extinction in the wild in the next decade.

Source: See Endnote 5 for this section.

warning of a potentially massive outbreak of disease in congested urban areas near factory farms. These farms are also easy targets for terrorists hoping to make food a weapon of mass destruction. One of the biggest vulnerabilities is the U.S. livestock industry, which has become progressively more disease-prone because of intensive factory-style conditions. With each farm housing tens of thousands of animals, operators are unable to monitor all stock regularly, making it hard to detect an outbreak before it spreads to the entire herd.[7] The rapid movement of products over long distances, from farms to

TABLE 2

Selected Animal Diseases That Can Spread to Humans

Disease	Human Impacts
Avian influenza	Jumped the species barrier for the first time in 1997, killing six people in Hong Kong. In 2003–05, the virulent H5N1 virus killed at least 50 people.
Nipah virus	Discovered in 1997 in Malaysia, where it spread from pigs to humans, causing a large outbreak of encephalitis; 93 percent of people infected had occupational exposure to pigs, and 105 people died.
Bovine spongiform encephalopathy (BSE, or mad cow disease)	Since its discovery in cattle in the United Kingdom in 1986, more than 30 other countries have reported cases of mad cow disease. Variant Creutzfeldt-Jakob disease (vCJD), the human form of the disease, has killed more than 150 people worldwide.

Source: See Endnote 6 for this section.

processing plants to consumers, further increases this risk. According to the U.S. Department of Agriculture, if foot-and-mouth disease were introduced in the United States, it could spread to 25 states in just five days.[8]

The following sections describe seven major public health concerns related to the growth of confined animal operations:

1. Avian Flu

Avian flu is just the most recent example of how animal diseases can undermine human health. Despite the heightened media attention, it is not a new disease, but one farmers have dealt with for centuries. Referred to as "fowl plague," it can spread from farm to farm and wipe out entire flocks of birds. Only during the last ten years, however, has the disease really changed, mutating into a form that can jump the species barrier and infect humans.[9]

The biggest and worst modern outbreak of avian flu began in Asia in 2003, and it continues to affect human health and poultry production in the region today. So far, all outbreaks of the highly pathogenic form of the disease have been caused by influenza-A viruses of subtypes H5 and H7. The current H5NI virus, the most virulent yet, has killed millions of chickens. The most common symptoms include swollen heads, reddish legs, and watery eyes. The virus spreads rapidly and strikes quickly, with a mortality rate for birds of almost 100 percent.[10]

According to the U.N. Food and Agriculture Organization, the spread of avian flu may have been facilitated by the rapid scaling-up of poultry and pig operations, and the massive geographic concentration of livestock, in China, Thailand, and Vietnam. In East and Southeast Asia alone, some 6 billion birds are raised for food, with major clusters of production located near the region's booming megacities, close to other livestock and humans.[11] The number of chickens in Thailand, Vietnam, and Indonesia has tripled since the 1980s, and China has doubled its poultry production in little more than 15 years, to 2 billion birds.[12] Asian consumers are getting more chicken and eggs in their diets than ever before, with demand doubling and tripling in some regions.[13] Consumption of duck meat is also rising, and experts believe this may have led to the spread of the most recent form of avian flu. Wild birds, especially ducks, have been called "trojan horses" because they are extremely efficient carriers of the disease (often remaining symptom-free) and can cover a wider area than domestic birds.[14]

Avian flu is not confined to birds, however. A 2005 study in *Science* found that tigers at a zoo in Thailand contracted the disease from eating raw poultry.[15] Domestic cats can also get avian flu and pass it to other cats, though there is no evidence yet that they can give it to humans.[16] Far more worrisome is the finding that avian flu can spread directly to pigs and to humans. In places with high concentrations of pigs and chickens, such as Asia, pigs can serve as a "mixing vessel" for the virus because of their genetic similarity to humans. In China, where half the world's pork is produced and consumed, pigs and chickens often live in close proximity to one another and to people on backyard farms or large factory farms.[17] As a result, avian influenza virus can combine with pig influenza to create an entirely different strain of the disease. According to Michael Osterholm, director of the Center for Infectious Disease Research and Policy at the University of Minnesota, "it's clear that Southeast Asia poses the greatest risk today of a new virus unfolding and coming forward as a pandemic strain. Darwin could not have created a more efficient re-assortment laboratory if he tried." [18]

Perhaps most disturbing is new evidence that bird flu can be transmitted directly from chickens and other birds to humans, without having to mix with strains of pig flu. Avian flu jumped the species barrier in Hong Kong in 1997, killing 6 of the 18 people infected. Since then, it has mutated into a strain that can be spread from birds to humans at least two more times. In 2003, avian flu struck the Netherlands, killing two people. Then in October 2004, the first probable human-to-human transmission was reported in Thailand, infecting at least two people and killing one. In total, more than 50 people have officially died from avian flu between 2003 and 2005, but countless other cases likely went undiagnosed. [19]

The virus continues to change. Although a 2004 study in China found that with every new outbreak, avian flu was becoming more lethal, that may no longer be the case. [20] After very high chicken and human mortality in Asia in 2004—up to 70 percent of people contracting the disease died—an outbreak in Vietnam in April 2005 triggered much lower human mortality, killing only about 20 percent of those infected. [21] Fewer chickens are also dying from the disease, but this isn't necessarily good news. According to the World Health Organization (WHO), the virus could be evolving to become "less virulent and more infectious," meaning that while it isn't as lethal, it could affect many more people. [22] Chickens may also be developing resistance to the disease and, like ducks, could spread it asymptomatically, making it harder to control and treat.

International health officials worry that the most recent and deadly strain of avian flu is now impossible to wipe out in Asian birds and may someday precipitate a global human flu pandemic. The real fear is that someone could be infected simultaneously with a human form of the influenza virus and with avian flu, giving the viruses the opportunity to mix,

COUNTRY STUDY 3

China

"If you ignore the stench and the contaminated soil and water," says David Brubaker, "it's like walking into a Fortune 500 company." Brubaker, an agribusiness consultant and an expert on factory farming, describes the entryways and offices of China's factory farms, some of which house more than 100,000 animals, as "palatial." But once you get inside, he notes, they are definitely not fit for royalty.

With more than 1.3 billion people, China leads the world in both production and consumption of meat. It alone accounts for most of the surge in demand for all animal products in the developing world, according to the International Food Policy Research Institute. Since 1983, domestic per capita meat and milk consumption have more than doubled.

Chinese government policy calls for a dramatic increase in the number of animals raised domestically, with the aim of doubling the value of animal production over the next 10 years. Factory farming is key to achieving this goal: already, China boasts an estimated 14,000 confined animal feeding operations, and about 15 percent of its pork and chicken production comes from factory farms. But not everyone in China supports the shift to industrial-style farming. While some provinces are willing to embrace factory farms as a way to improve the economy, others are resistant to the idea of raising animals in industrial operations, says Brubaker.

In southern China, some officials are reluctant to encourage factory farming because of the risk of animal diseases, which can spread rapidly in tropical climates. They also worry about the threat to human health posed by large pig, duck, and chicken farms in close proximity to one another and to big cities. In the cooler northern regions, where the risk of disease is lower, a leading concern is water. Raising large numbers of animals in confined conditions requires huge water inputs, but there isn't much to spare, as regional water tables have fallen precipitously in recent years.

China's State Environment Protection Administration reports that industrial farms are a major source of pollution as well. Chinese livestock produced more than 1.7 billion tons of manure in 1995, much of it originating on small farms and used to fertilize crops. A large share of the waste from the rapidly growing factory farms, however, ends up in the country's rivers. In central China, where pig and chicken farms produce 40 times as much nitrogen as all other regional factories combined, livestock waste has contributed to eutrophication of the Yangtze Delta.

As industrial animal production grows, producers in China will be confronted with a new set of social and environmental concerns. With its strong central government, however, China has a unique opportunity to avert many of the problems that have occurred elsewhere—for instance, by requiring large farms to tighten environmental controls and improve animal welfare, and by encouraging a shift to smaller-scale, grass-fed, and organic livestock production.

Sources: See Endnote 3a, p. 85.

mutate, and spread to the human population. Because the resulting virus would be fast-moving and easily transmittable, experts fear that it could be more lethal than AIDS. WHO estimates that if a pandemic occurred, between 2 million and 50 million people could die, affecting 20–50 percent of the global population, depending on the level of preparedness.[23]

The effects can be devastating for human and bird populations alike. When avian flu first struck in 2003–04, FAO, WHO, and the World Organization for Animal Health (OIE) advised killing all birds on farms near an outbreak as one of the only effective means of control.[24] More than 140 million birds in Asia have been "depopulated" since the outbreak first hit.[25] Unfortunately, gathering birds into plastic bags and, in some cases, burying or burning them alive did little to prevent the disease from spreading. As a result, FAO and OIE reversed their decision in 2005, saying that "for ethical, ecological and economical reasons," culling should no longer be used as a primary means of control.[26] Instead FAO and OIE have urged countries to vaccinate chickens, a highly effective, but also very expensive, method of controlling the disease.[27]

Although the unsanitary conditions, close concentration, and genetic uniformity of animals in large factory farms may have helped facilitate the emergence and spread of avian flu, it is the smaller producers who are most devastated economically by the disease. Thailand, for example, was the world's fourth largest poultry exporter before the outbreak occurred.[28] The country lost millions of dollars in export profits, and many small farmers have been forced to abandon poultry production. According to Emmanuelle Guerne-Ble-ich of FAO, these farmers, who typically own anywhere from

15–50 chickens and use them as an "insurance policy" in times of need—selling them for food, medicine, or other necessities—are "amongst the worst affected and least able to recover" from the outbreak.[29]

Unfortunately, officials from FAO and WHO are recommending, at least in the short term, moving all poultry production to large farms and eliminating free-range production altogether. In April 2005, Vietnam imposed a ban on live poultry markets and began requiring farms to convert to factory-style farming methods in 15 cities and provinces, including Ho Chi Minh City and Hanoi.[30] Thailand, too, plans to impose restrictions on free-range poultry. By implementing expensive control measures, including isolating animals by type on farms, separating chicks from parents, and getting market vendors to segregate chickens, ducks, and pigs, officials hope to curtail the spread of the disease.[31] Although this could drive thousands more small producers out of business and eliminate traditional means of food production, it may be the only way, at least for now, for some countries to prevent the further spread of avian flu and its threat to human health.

2. Bovine spongiform encephalopathy (BSE)

Bovine spongiform encephalopathy, also called "mad cow disease," is another well-known example of the perils of industrial meat production. But rather than emerging in the wild, as avian flu did, experts speculate that BSE first originated in the feed-processing plants of the United Kingdom. In addition to giving their livestock grain, hormones, and antibiotics, farmers can make animals gain weight quickly by feeding them the bits and pieces of other animals discarded during processing, including nervous tissue, bone, and blood. Scientists suspect that mad cow disease emerged in the 1980s when sheep infected with scrapie, a disease similar to mad cow, were fed to cattle that were in turn rendered and fed back to other cattle, amplifying and spreading the disease. Scrapie in sheep, BSE in cattle, and chronic wasting disease in elk and deer are all caused by prions, rogue proteins that make their way into the brain and poke it with holes, destroying normal cells and causing animals to stumble, show aggression, and eventually die.[32]

Unfortunately, mad cow disease itself isn't destroyed when the animals die—it can later spread to humans who eat meat from infected animals. Since 1986, when BSE was first detected in the United Kingdom, it has been found in at least 34 other countries, including Japan, Spain, Italy, France, Canada, and most recently the United States. Health officials estimate that more than 150 people have died from variant Creutzfeldt-Jakob disease (vCJD), the human form of mad cow.[33]

Although the practice of feeding cattle the meat and bone meal of ruminants has been banned in the United Kingdom and other nations, it is impossible to predict how many people may have eaten beef infected with BSE or might eventually contract vCJD. One study estimates that more than 3,800 people could get the disease.[34] Moreover, scientists still do not know the incubation period of BSE and whether the risk of developing vCJD depends on the quantity of meat consumed or on the frequency of consumption. Before 1996, meat and bone meal from the United Kingdom was shipped all over the world, to at least 12 nations in Africa as well as to the United States and most European, Middle Eastern, and Asian nations.[35]

In 2001, the Japanese government took the unprecedented step of requiring that all cattle raised in the country be tested for mad cow disease before slaughter, though this blanket policy was eased in August 2005.[36] Japan also banned beef imports from the United States in 2003 in an effort to protect consumers. That move was highly controversial and, as of July 2005, U.S. officials were still trying to persuade the country to re-open its markets to American beef. Despite these efforts, Japan may be in the midst of a mad cow epidemic. To date, 20 Japanese cattle have been discovered with the disease.[37]

Many countries still lack the necessary regulations—and political will—to prevent mad cow disease in cattle. In the United States, the Department of Agriculture (USDA) repeatedly assured the public that the risk to animal and human health was non-existent. Then, in late 2003, the first case of BSE was discovered in Washington state, costing the U.S. beef industry $3.2–$4.7 billion in 2004 alone, according to a study at Kansas State University.[38] Alternatively, if the U.S. had begun testing one-quarter of all cattle meant for export for BSE when the disease was first discovered, and if no further cases had been detected and markets re-opened, beef producers would have profited by $750 million, reports the study.

In June 2005, a second U.S. cow slaughtered in 2004 was retested and found to be infected.[39] Despite USDA assurances that the animal never entered the human or animal feed chains and that this was an isolated case, it is likely not the last incidence of BSE to be found in the United States. Some consumer activists claim that the country has been able to hide other cases of mad cow by using ineffective testing procedures (the most accurate measure, the Western Blot test, was not used in the U.S. until 2005) and by failing to test the millions of cattle slaughtered each year.[40]

As with avian flu, different strains of BSE exist. In 2003, researchers in Italy discovered there may be "more than one way to make a cow mad."[41] Unlike BSE, this possible new strain—called BASE, for bovine amyloidotic spongiform encephalopathy—has appeared in cows showing no symptoms, making it harder for slaughterhouse inspectors to detect the disease before slaughter. Researchers do not yet know if BASE can spread to humans, but experts suspect it may be responsible for certain cases of Creutzfeld-Jakob disease that seemed to occur spontaneously. Until they know for sure, scientists in Italy are calling for more stringent testing of cows for both BSE and BASE.

BSE is not just a threat to cattle. In January 2005, French researchers discovered that a goat slaughtered in 2002 tested positive for the disease, marking the first time it has been found in other livestock.[42] Scientists with the European Union are declining to say whether goat flesh is safe to consume or not, but have agreed to more testing of the 12 million goats in EU member countries.[43]

Researchers once believed that humans could contract vCJD only from eating the brain, spinal cord, or other nervous tissue of cattle infected with BSE. But a Swiss study published in *Science* in 2005 found prions in the liver, kidney, and pancreas of rodents. This suggests, according to Adriano Aguzzi, lead researcher of the study, that there is "reason to reappraise...the regulations that are already in place" to protect humans from infected meat.[44] That may mean eating no beef products at all or choosing only organic or pasture-raised beef products.

3. Foot-and-Mouth Disease

Foot-and-mouth disease (FMD) is another animal disease made famous in the United Kingdom. In early 2001, the U.K. slaughtered and burned nearly 600,000 cattle, 3.2 million sheep, and thousands of pigs, goats, and other animals exposed to the disease, a highly contagious virus that affects cloven-hoofed animals.[45] Just recovering from the mad cow scare, the British beef industry lost £9 billion (US$16 billion) in revenue.[46]

Unlike BSE, FMD is rarely fatal to animals. It is considered widespread in many regions of the world, including parts of Africa, Europe, and Asia. Until recently, most nations could control the disease and keep it within their borders. But with the scaling-up and concentration of beef production, things have changed. One reason a 1967 FMD outbreak in the United Kingdom didn't spread nearly so widely or quickly is that animals didn't travel as far between farms and slaughterhouses. The number of cattle abattoirs in England, Wales, and Scotland has declined dramatically since the 1970s, from nearly 2,000 in 1972 to some 277 today, forcing producers to transport their animals farther.[47] Worldwide, some 44 million animals are transported across borders each year, and millions more are transported long distances by truck and rail within countries.[48]

4. Nipah Virus

Nipah virus is one of the newest zoonoses—diseases that can jump from animals to humans—to be discovered. It is a perfect, albeit complex, example of what can happen when big agriculture combines with the destruction of fragile ecosystems. Nipah was first discovered in 1997 in a small Malaysian village, home to one of the largest pig farms in the country. Nearby residents began coming down with flu-like symptoms, and more than 100 of them died. Epidemiologists eventually figured out that the disease originated in bats, which spread it to pigs and then to humans.[49] But how?

The scenario goes like this: in 1997, forest fires in Borneo and Sumatra precipitated by El Niño forced thousands of fruit bats to search for food in nearby Malaysia. Many of them visited fruit trees that towered over newly established large pig farms, dripping their saliva and half-eaten fruit into the stalls below. Although bats are not sickened by Nipah, in pigs it causes a severe coughing sickness, allowing the virus to spread efficiently to humans through the air.[50]

Peter Daszak, Executive Director of Wildlife Trust's Consortium for Conservation Medicine, notes that the growth of massive-scale pig farming likely played an important role in the emergence of Nipah virus. "Without these large, intensively managed pig farms in Malaysia, it would have been extremely difficult for the virus to emerge," he says.[51] In April 2004, Nipah struck again, this time in Bangladesh, killing up to 74 percent of its human victims.[52] Scientists predict that as industrial agriculture continues to move into tropical environments, the risk of Nipah-like viruses and other diseases that can jump the species barrier is growing.

5. Food-borne Illness

Industrial meat production can lead to less exotic, but no less serious, public health problems. In 1993, four children died from eating hamburgers from two Jack-in-the-Box fast food restaurants in California and Washington state.[53] Every year, the United States recalls millions of tons of chicken, beef, and pork products because of potential food safety concerns. The most common food-borne infections caused by contaminated meat and food include campylobacter, listeria, salmonella, cryptosporidium, and pathogenic *E. coli*.[54] (See Table 3.)

Although consumers have long been blamed for cooking meat improperly and practicing poor hygiene in the kitchen, the truth is that contamination of meat products often happens long before they reach the consumer. Raising animals in crowded conditions, says Ian Langford of the University of East Anglia, encourages the growth and spread of microorganisms

TABLE 3

Selected Food-borne Pathogens

Pathogen	Description
Campylobacter	The most common food-borne infection in the United States. Half of infections are associated with eating contaminated poultry or handling chickens.
Listeria	Present in soft cheese and meat pastes. For healthy adults, it may cause no symptoms at all, but among pregnant women, infants, the elderly, and the ill, the death rate is about 30 percent.
Parasites	Amoebas—parasites spread by contaminated food and water—cause 100,000 deaths a year, second only to malaria in mortality due to parasites.
Pathogenic E. coli	Caused by eating food that has come into contact with fecal matter. Responsible for up to 25 percent of all cases of diarrhea among children and infants in the developing world.
Salmonella	Spread primarily through raw or undercooked eggs, poultry, and milk. Accounts for the greatest proportion of food-borne disease in industrial countries.

Source: See Endnote 54 for this section.

in meat because animals often arrive at the slaughterhouse covered in feces. "The problem," according to Langford, "isn't with the consumer looking after the food well enough, but...in the food production process."[55]

E. coli 0157:H7 is one infection usually caused when meat comes into contact with fecal matter. But how does this happen? As Eric Schlosser writes in his best-selling book *Fast Food Nation*, "changes in how cattle are raised, slaughtered and processed have created an ideal means for the pathogen to spread."[56] Cattle are packed tightly into feedlots where they stand in pools of manure, allowing the disease to recirculate in troughs and survive in manure for as long as three months.

But it's in the modern slaughterhouses where E. coli is most efficiently spread. Because animal hides are covered in manure, it's hard to keep fecal matter from coming in contact with the animal's flesh. In addition, when workers pull out the intestines of cattle, there is often what is called "spillage"—literally the contents of the animal's digestive system spill everywhere. And modern slaughter and processing techniques frequently sacrifice food safety for speed: workers on high-velocity production lines may gut 60 or more animals an hour, making it easy for contamination to spread.[57]

6. Antibiotic Resistance

In 1998, something happened to a 12-year old Nebraska boy that has since become increasingly common. That April, the boy, the son of a veterinarian who also raised cattle on the family's farm, came down with a bad case of diarrhea, fever, and abdominal pain. Doctors determined that he had salmonella, a leading bacterial cause of food poisoning and the culprit behind 1.4 million food poisoning cases and some 500 deaths each year in the United States alone. Unfortunately, the boy's infection failed to respond to a first round of antibiotics. Then another antibiotic didn't work and then another and another. In all, the bacterium was resistant to 13 different antibiotics, including ceftriaxone, an important drug for treating salmonella in children, and ceftiofur, an antibiotic used for animals. Intrigued by the strength of the infection and by the ineffectiveness of the drugs, researchers at the University of Illinois discovered that the boy's multi-resistant strain of salmonella was the same kind found in cattle on his parents' farm and on three other farms where his father had treated cattle.[58]

Because of the practice of using antibiotics in animal agriculture, food-borne infections and other human diseases are becoming harder to fight. When people consume animal products containing resistant bacteria, the human gut acts as a breeding ground for antibiotic resistance, spreading the problem from one species to another. The results can be lethal. For example, a 2005 study in the *Journal of Infectious Diseases* found that patients with antibiotic-resistant infections caused by salmonella bacteria are more likely to suffer potentially deadly bloodstream infections than patients with non-resistant salmonella. The study notes that the resistance in the bacteria results chiefly from the use of antibiotics in food animals.[59]

The overuse of antibiotics in animal agriculture can have

other surprising human-health effects, including increased incidence of antibiotic-resistant urinary tract infections (UTIs). Scientists at the University of California at Berkeley recently reported that an outbreak of resistant UTIs in 2004 was probably caused by food-borne bacteria, and that this resistance likely arose from antibiotic use in agricultural animals.[60] UTIs are the most common bacteria infection in women, leading to some 8 million physician visits and nearly 250,000 related kidney infections a year in the United States alone.[61] When UTIs fail to respond to standard antibiotic treatments, delays in finding an effective alternative can prolong the disease and lead to medical complications, including permanent kidney damage.

It's hard to believe, but in the United States, livestock consume eight times more antibiotics by volume than humans do, according to a report by the Union of Concerned Scientists (UCS).[62] Antimicrobial drugs have been given routinely to animals in their feed and water since the 1950s. For reasons scientists can't fully explain, these low levels of antimicrobial drugs allow animals to gain weight faster on less feed.[63] UCS estimates, using data from several government and industry sources, that between 1985 and 2000 the amount of antimicrobial drugs used non-therapeutically on American livestock rose by 50 percent. Beef cattle now receive 28 percent more antibiotics than they did in the 1980s, and antimicrobial use and dependence on tetracyclines by pig producers, who administer the drug mainly in the weeks before slaughter, has risen 15 percent over this period. On a per-bird basis, antimicrobial use by poultry producers has risen 307 percent since the 1980s.[64]

Many of these antibiotics are very similar to, or the same as, those used to fight human disease, including penicillin, tetracycline, and erythromycin. But while people usually need a doctor's prescription for antibiotics to treat a specific ailment, in agriculture the drugs are typically used in the absence of disease. Owners of CAFOs are allowed to dose entire flocks or herds to promote increased growth or to prevent diseases that might result when too many animals are housed in a poorly-ventilated, enclosed area. The animals then excrete the antimicrobials in their waste, and when people eat meat, they get an

COUNTRY STUDY 4

India

In 1971, a flood swept over India, but it wasn't caused by the annual monsoons. Rather, it was created by thousands of small-scale milk producers as part of a project to jumpstart milk production in the country and boost incomes for poor farmers. Operation Flood, as it was called, brought about a "white revolution," increasing milk production from just 21 million metric tons in 1961 to more than 80 million metric tons today, making India the largest milk producer in the world.

Funded in part by the World Bank and administered by India's National Dairy Board, Operation Flood started out by focusing on small producers with one or two cows. The program established new links between rural producers and urban consumers and helped to address both the risks modern milk-processing plants faced in using smallholder milk and the difficulties many farmers had in getting their milk to market.

Today, however, this focus on the productivity of smaller-scale producers may be under threat. India has one of the most deregulated dairy industries in the world, and experts fear that globalization, as well as rising demand for dairy products in India, will lead to bigger farms and more industrialized production methods, driving smallholders out of business and creating environmental problems.

Although India is typically thought of as a predominantly vegetarian country because of Hindu beliefs in the sacredness of cows, production of non-beef animal products is growing rapidly. For example, India now ranks fifth in the world in both broiler and egg production. Much of this production is occurring in large factory farms near densely populated cities, exacerbating concerns about the health and environmental risks.

Sources: See Endnote 4a, p. 85.

---

unexpected dose of drugs. According to Dr. David Wallinga, an expert on antibiotics at the Institute for Agriculture and Trade Policy, "we're sacrificing a future where antibiotics will work for treating sick people by squandering them today for animals that are not sick at all."[65]

But eating meat tainted with antibiotics isn't the only way to spread resistant pathogens. In a 2004 study in *Environmental Health Perspectives*, scientists reported that air samples collected from a pig CAFO contained multidrug-resistant strains of three different bacteria—Enterococcus, coagulase-negative staphylococci, and viridans group streptococci—all of which are associated with a variety of human infections.[66] Ninety-eight percent of the isolated samples were resistant to at least two antibiotics important in human treatments, including erythromycin, clindamycin, virginiamycin, and tetracycline. None, however, were resistant to vancomycin, an antibiotic that has never been approved for use in pigs in the United States.

The effects of antimicrobial use in animal production are cropping up in other countries as well. A 2001 study by Compassion in World Farming South Africa found that contaminated meat from slaughtered hens contained the same infectious disease bacteria that had appeared in people in the surrounding community.[67] The bacteria were 100-percent resistant to the most commonly used antibiotics. In Thailand, meanwhile, workers in pig and chicken farms have been found to be infected with antibiotic-resistant salmonella and *E. coli*.[68]

Because of the importance of antimicrobials in human medicine, the European Union has prohibited all growth-promoting uses of antibiotics in animals since 1998.[69] Indiscriminate use of antibiotics in agriculture, according to the World Health Organization, poses a significant health threat.[70] And a 2001 study in the *Journal of the American Medical Association* states that as the armory of effective antibiotics erodes, "there appear to be few, if any, new classes of drugs in clinical development."[71]

Yet instead of calling for changes in the way animals are raised and meat is processed, many producers and government officials have proposed simply irradiating meat to kill food-borne pathogens and bacteria. Irradiation can increase shelf-life and kill insects and food-borne pests. It can also mask the filth that results from factory-style production methods. Unfortunately, studies show that irradiated food is less nutritious than non-irradiated food. And because the process involves radiation, eating irradiated meat may encourage chromosomal abnormalities as well as cancer.[72]

7. Hormones and Other Toxins

Hormones can enter the food chain as well, modifying the meat and milk people eat. As with antibiotics, producers found after World War II that certain hormones, including testosterone, progesterone, and their synthetic equivalents (trenbolone acetate, zeranol, 17 beta-estradiol, and melengestrol acetate), can increase an animal's weight and milk production. Hormones can boost animal growth by 20 percent, while costing only a few dollars a head. In the United States, as much as two-thirds of beef cattle are treated with hormones, either by injection or through implants. And one-third of dairy cows are given recombinant bovine growth hormone (rBGH) to increase milk production, despite the fact that conventional producers in the U.S. currently face extremely low prices because of overproduction.[73]

But these drugs don't just fatten animals. They end up in the meat and dairy products people consume, leading to a variety of health problems. Because of the potential side-effects of hormones, including breast and intestinal cancers and premature puberty, the European Union banned their use in 1988 and has prohibited imports of U.S. and Canadian beef, which still contains the drugs.[74]

Other hazards, including arsenic, dioxin, polychlorinated biphenyls (PCBs), and a range of other persistent organic pollutants, can show up in industrial meat. Arsenic, mixed with antibiotics and feed to promote growth and prevent illness, is fed to 70 percent of chickens in the United States, where it can be found as residue in meat.[75] And dioxins and PCBs released from industrial processes make their way into animal fat, with potential human-health effects. Both dioxin and PCBs are known human carcinogens, and even low-level exposure to dioxin could have adverse reproductive and developmental impacts.[76] These chemicals are also present in fish.[77] The higher up the food chain we eat, the more exposure we have to them, especially if our food comes from factory farms.

Food-safety outbreaks and contamination problems aside, there are other reasons to avoid factory-farmed meat. Nutritionists have found that livestock fed with grain are not as healthy and nutritious as the grass-fed alternative. A 2002 study in the *European Journal of Clinical Nutrition* found that meat from grass-fed livestock not only contained substantially less fat than grain-fed meat, but the fat it did contain was also much healthier.[78] Grass-fed meat contains Omega-3 fatty acids, like those found in certain fish, which help lower cholesterol.[79] In contrast, animals raised in feedlots accumulate Omega-6 fatty acids, the bad fats, which have been linked to cancer, diabetes, obesity, and immune disorders.[80]

Grass-fed products also have higher levels of conjugated linoleic acid, which can block tumor growth and lower the risk of obesity and other diseases.[81] And eggs from free-range hens contain up to 30 percent more vitamin E, 50 percent more folic acid, and 30 percent more vitamin B-12 than factory eggs, while the yolk holds higher levels of antioxidant carotenes.[82] Beef from cattle raised in feedlots on growth hormones and high-grain diets, in contrast, contains lower levels of vitamins A, D, E, and beta carotene, and twice as much fat as grass-fed beef.[83]

While the world's poorest people might in fact benefit from the addition of small amounts of meat and other animal products to their diets, consumers in both rich and developing nations alike may be experiencing the ill-effects of eating too much meat. Although past studies pointed to a tenuous link between high red-meat consumption and cancer, more recent research suggests that there may indeed be serious health risks. A 2005 study in the *Journal of the American Medical Association*, which tracked subjects over many years, found that people who ate large amounts of processed meats had twice the risk of developing colon cancer as those who ate the least meat.[84] And those who ate the most red meat had a 40 percent chance of contracting rectal cancer. Meanwhile, a 2003 study reported that women who consume high-meat diets may be at greater risk for breast cancer than those who eat fewer animal-derived saturated fats.[85]

Even more surprising, however, is that these health problems are also occurring in transitional and developing countries. According to Dr. Barry Popkin, a nutrition expert at the University of North Carolina, the shift to greater consumption of animal foods has been fueled in part by the declining price of beef and other meats, as well as lower prices for feed grains.[86] The world price of beef per 100 kilograms has fallen to about 25 percent of its value 30 years ago. These lower prices have allowed for a rapid increase in the amount of meat—and by extension, saturated fats—people are eating and, according to Popkin, "represent a major factor behind the global pandemic of obesity."[87] In many developing countries, incidence of overweight and obesity is reaching levels rivaling those of the United States. More than 300 million adults worldwide are obese, and 115 million people in developing countries suffer from obesity-related health problems.[88] On the other hand, people who eat little or no meat have significantly lower body mass indexes (BMIs) than those who eat more meat, according to a study of Swedish women by Tufts University.[89]

Lower prices and greater meat demand have also helped fast-food chains saturate the developing world, widening the availability of animal products. Between 1996 and 2001, the number of McDonald's restaurants in Africa, Asia, the Middle East, and the Pacific grew an astounding 126 percent.[90] KFC has been particularly successful in China, opening more than 1,000 stores over the last few years.[91] In India, the fast-food industry is growing by some 40 percent a year and was expected to generate more than $1 billion in 2004.[92] In most cases, the products offered at these chains are extremely high in saturated fat and cholesterol and contain very few nutrients.

Happier Meals

Given the problems caused by factory farming—and the strong protests these have inspired—the meat and livestock industries are finding increasingly creative solutions. In 1999, researchers in Canada developed a novel way to control pollution from pig farms: genetically engineering pigs to produce less-noxious manure. Called "Enviro-pigs," these animals contain chromosomes inserted from mice and a type of bacteria and produce manure that contains 75 percent less phosphorous than non-engineered pigs.[1] As a result, say researchers, this fertilizer is better suited for agricultural applications because it will be less polluting.

Biotechnology offers other so-called "solutions" for the problems caused by factory farming. At industrial dairy operations that use milking machines, where conditions can be unsanitary, cows often suffer from mastitis, a painful bacterial infection that causes inflammation and swelling of the udders (a problem, in fact, exacerbated by a previous biotech solution, the use of bovine growth hormone). Mastitis costs the U.S. dairy industry billions of dollars a year in treatment and lost production. But rather than addressing the conditions that perpetuate the disease, researchers with the U.S. Department of Agriculture have introduced a gene into dairy cows that enables them to produce a protein that kills the bacteria.[2] Some biotech companies are even cloning livestock for meat production, claiming the animals can be raised better in labs than on farms.

These end-of-the-pipe remedies are certainly innovative, but they don't address the real problem. Factory farming is an inefficient, ecologically disruptive, dangerous, and inhumane way of making meat.

But let's try to imagine, as writer Michael Pollan has suggested, if factory farms and slaughterhouses were housed under glass, giving the public a view of what goes on inside.[3] Operations that treated their workers and animals with respect and recognized livestock's ecological role would produce a healthier product and have a far less destructive impact on the planet. Although this new relationship with meat will mean that there is not as much beef, chicken, and pork available for people in the industrial world, the meat will be better quality and better for us than the choices we have now.

Farmers everywhere are rising to the challenge of producing healthier, more environmentally sustainable meat products, while enjoying a range of unexpected benefits. For example, like most pigs in the mid-western United States, the more than 200 sows that live on Paul Willis's farm in Iowa love to eat corn. But Willis's animals have a diet and lifestyle very different from the other 15 million hogs raised in that state. Along with the grain they eat on a daily basis, Willis's hogs graze outside on pastures and are not confined in the concrete factories that dominate American pork production. Not only do the animals get the chance to exhibit their natural and instinctive behaviors, like rooting for food, playing, and nest-making, but the meat they produce is healthier and better-tasting than the pork produced on factory farms.[4]

Because pigs thrive under these more natural conditions, Willis can raise his meat without the use of antibiotics or growth promoters, lowering costs. And instead of selling his meat to Smithfield or one of the other big corporations that dominate U.S. hog production, Willis markets his pork through the Niman Ranch, a California-based company started in 1982 to distribute humanely-raised meat products to consumers and restaurants. Willis is part of a growing movement of farmers and consumers helping livestock go back to their roots.[5]

On the other side of the world, Bobby Inocencio, a farmer in the Philippines, is up against some powerful forces. His government doesn't see the growth of factory farming as a threat. To the contrary, many officials hope it will be a solution to their country's economic woes, and they're making it easier for large farms to dominate livestock production. For instance, the Department of Agriculture appears to have turned a blind eye when many farms have violated environmental and animal welfare regulations. The government has also encouraged large farms to expand by giving them loans. But as the farms get bigger and produce more, domestic prices for chicken and pork fall, forcing more farmers to scale up their production methods. And because the Philippines, like many other nations, is prevented by the General Agreement on Tariffs and Trade and the World Trade Organization from imposing tariffs on imports, the country is forced to open its market to cheap, factory-farmed American pork and poultry, which is then sold at lower prices than domestic meat.[6]

But Inocencio and others like him are hoping to change all that by helping farmers transform the way many Filipinos produce and eat chicken. Once a factory farmer, Inocencio raised white chickens for Pure Foods, one of the largest companies in the Philippines, and followed the standard model of squeezing tens of thousands of birds into cage-lined buildings. But in 1997, he decided to revive village-level poultry enterprises that support family-size farms. He began raising free-range chickens and teaching other farmers how to do the same. His birds roam freely in large tree-covered areas of his farm that he encloses using recycled fishing nets.[7]

Inocencio's farm is profitable in part because his costs per bird are considerably lower: no antibiotics, growth promoters, pricey feed, or huge sheds to maintain. But he has also found a niche in the Filipino market by giving consumers a taste of how things used to be. His chickens are part native and part Sasso (a French breed) and are better adapted to the local climate, unlike white chickens that are vulnerable to heat. Not only are Inocencio's chickens raised humanely, they are nutritious and taste good. They are just 5 percent fat, compared with 35 percent for white chicken, and they don't contain any antibiotics.[8]

Rafael Mariano, a leader in the Peasant Movement for the Philippines (KMP), is also aware of the problems caused by factory farming. He and the 800,000 farmers he works with believe that "factory farming is not acceptable, we have our own farming." But farmers, he says, are told by big agribusiness companies that their methods are old-fashioned, and that to compete in the global market they must forget what they have learned from generations of farming.[9]

Mariano and KMP are working to promote traditional methods of livestock production that benefit small farmers and increase local food security. This means doing what farmers used to do: raising both crops and animals. In mixed crop–livestock farms, animals and crops are parts of a self-sustaining system. Some farmers in the Philippines raise hogs, chickens, tilapia, and rice on the same farm. The manure from the hogs and chickens is used to fertilize the algae in ponds needed for tilapia and rice production. These farms generate little waste, provide a variety of foods, and give farmers security when prices for poultry, pork, and rice drop.[10]

COUNTRY STUDY 5

Brazil

In 2004, the United States Department of Agriculture identified Brazil as an emerging threat to U.S. agricultural dominance. Why? Because Brazil, long known for its prized beef exports, is now the second-largest producer of poultry in the world, just behind the U.S., and is fast becoming a leader in pork production as well.

Fueling this livestock growth is beans, beans, and more beans. Brazil is the world's second-largest producer of soybeans, a significant source of protein for animal feed, and this expanding production has enabled companies to erect huge chicken farms and piggeries in some of the most remote regions. In the town of Diamintino in Mato Grosso state, U.S.-based Smithfield Foods and a Brazilian partner have built one of the world's biggest pig farms, home to more than 150,000 animals. Set back from the highway and far from any neighbors who might complain about the smell or water pollution, the farm covers nearly 1,000 hectares and cost $24 billion to build, according to a 2004 article in the *Chicago Tribune*. More than a dozen waste lagoons are located on the premises, and the manure is distributed free to local farmers for use as fertilizer.

Despite the potential environmental and public health problems created by Brazil's factory-farm boom, many European nations will actually benefit from the increased production. How? Under the recently adopted Kyoto Protocol, polluters in industrial nations can offset their own emissions by financing greenhouse gas-saving technologies in the developing world. The Irish company AgCert is now installing methane-capture technology at 30 Brazilian pig farms, and hopes to sell the emissions reductions from the improved manure handling to industrial polluters, governments, and energy traders on the international market. The emissions offset potential is huge: in the state of Minas Gerais alone, 3.4 million pigs produce 7 million tons of waste per year.

Sources: See Endnote 5a, p. 85.

Despite the growing popularity of grass-fed beef in the United States, less than 1 percent of the 33 million cattle slaughtered there each year are pasture-raised.[11] But that's changing. In just the last four years, the number of U.S. farms raising grass-fed beef has grown from 50 to over 1,000—thanks, in part, to farmers and entrepreneurs like Steffen Schneider of Hawthorne Valley Farms in New York.[12] According to Schneider, who is raising cattle on pasture, "one of the biggest crimes of industrial agriculture is that we've moved all the animals off the land."[13]

Much of the credit for the growing popularity of organic and grass-fed meat goes to Joel Salatin, who began raising cattle and chickens on pasture in the 1970s. Today, Salatin's Polyface Farm in Virginia is a mecca for farmers who want to learn how to raise grass-fed and pasture-raised beef, chicken, turkey, and lamb.[14]

One of the biggest benefits of raising animals on pasture is that it is less environmentally destructive. Because grass is their primary food source, the cattle require little or no grain, eliminating the environmental costs of growing soybeans and corn with chemical fertilizers, as well as the energy costs of shipping grain to feedlots. Grass farming also helps preserve native grasses and control erosion, and it eliminates the need for pesticides.[15] Overgrazing, however, can be catastrophic, especially if it is done in biologically fragile regions like Brazil's Amazon forest.[16] (See Sidebar 3, page 58.)

It's not just the producers, but the people who slaughter and package meat, who are choosing to strengthen and reestablish more humane and environmentally responsible methods. Since 1995, the number of small meat-processing plants in the United States, many of which are family owned and operated, has declined by 10 percent, according to the American Association of Meat Processors.[17] One reason for the decline is that smaller processors are held to the same standards as the meat-processing giants—a one-size-fits-all regulatory approach that fails to differentiate between operations that slaughter a few cattle a week from those that process thousands of animals a week. As a result, the smaller players are forced out, making it hard for farmers raising organic and pasture-raised meat to find someone to take their animals.

But Heifer International, an organization best known for working with small livestock farmers in developing countries, is hoping to keep small producers in business by helping communities find ways to fund the construction of more slaughterhouses and processing facilities, while also educating

SIDEBAR 3

Eating Up the Forests

Cattle and bison are often an important part of grassland and forest ecosystems, helping to maintain plant diversity and control the spread of invasive species. But livestock overgrazing can have disastrous consequences. In the 1980s, environmentalists in the United States and other industrial countries blamed McDonald's and other fast-food chains for buying beef raised in what was once lush rainforest in Central and South America. Indeed, since 1970, farmers and ranchers have destroyed thousands of hectares of biologically rich forests in the region. But contrary to environmentalists' claims, most of the meat produced at the time was not for export, but for domestic consumption.

Today, that is changing. For the first time ever, the growth in Brazilian cattle production—80 percent of which is in the Amazon—is largely export-driven. Brazilian beef exports tripled between 1995 and 2003, to US$1.5 billion, according to the U.S. Department of Agriculture. The share of Europe's processed meat imports originating in Brazil increased from 40 percent to 74 percent from 1990 to 2001. Markets in Russia and the Middle East are also responsible for much of this new demand.

According to a 2004 report by the Center for International Forestry Research (CIFOR), rapid growth in Brazilian beef sales overseas has accelerated destruction of the Amazon rainforest. The total area of forest lost increased from 41.5 million hectares in 1990 to 58.7 million hectares in 2000. In just 10 years, says CIFOR, an area twice the size of Portugal was lost, most of it to pasture. "In a nutshell," says David Kaimowitz, director general of CIFOR, "cattle ranchers are making mincemeat out of Brazil's Amazon rainforests."

A June 2005 report from FAO also concludes that cattle ranching is the main cause of forest destruction in Latin America. The report predicts that by 2010, more than 1.2 million hectares of forest will be lost in Central America, while in South America 18 million hectares of forest will disappear because of clearing land for grazing cattle.

Soybean production for animal feed is leading to the destruction of Brazil's forests as well. By the end of 2004, more than 16,000 kilometers of rainforest were cleared for farming, a 6-percent increase over 2003, and most of that was to grow soybeans to feed Brazil's rapidly growing poultry and pork industries. Like beef, most of the meat produced is not for Brazilian dinner tables, but for export.

But producing meat in Brazil doesn't have to harm the environment. In the country's Pantanal region, home to the world's largest floodplain, farmers are learning to raise certified organic beef and to preserve the region's native grasses. Funded by U.S.-based Conservation International and Brazil's Biodynamic Beef Institute, farmers from six cattle ranches, covering 162,000 hectares, are switching from conventional to organic beef. To become certified, they can't use any antibiotics or growth hormones or destroy any of the local vegetation for grazing, and they must raise only native breeds, adapted to the region's climate and vegetation. By raising cattle in a way that is compatible with the surrounding environment, farmers aren't forced to destroy the environment.

Sources: See Endnote 16 for this section.

consumers and farmers about the benefits of locally produced meat. According to Terry Wollen, Director of Animal Well-Being at Heifer, one of the biggest obstacles small producers face is not having enough animals to bring to the big facilities, which are used to dealing with large numbers of animals. To address this problem, Heifer is working with producers to find ways to work with local and state governmental agencies to make the rules more accommodating for small producers.[18]

One way small producers can stay in business is by finding a market for locally and humanely raised animal products. Not far from where Iowa farmer Paul Willis raises his pigs, for example, customers at Sioux City's Floyd Boulevard Local Foods Market can get a taste of something special. The market, started in 2004 by two women concerned about the welfare of farm animals in Iowa, in partnership with the Humane Society of the United States, guarantees that the meat, milk, and eggs sold by local producers are raised humanely and in accordance with the natural functions of the animal. Instead of gestations crates for sows, battery cages for hens, and veal crates for calves, says Penny Price Fee, one of the market's founders, all the animals sold at the market are raised without antibiotics, are free-range, and are treated humanely throughout their lives.[19] Although prices are a little higher than at the grocery store, customers get a range of side benefits for the bison steaks, free-range eggs, and hormone-free milk they buy at the market. For example, says Price Fee, the bison raised by the Mason Family are restoring the area's native grasslands by eating invasive species. Customers also get the satisfaction of knowing that the animals they're eating didn't suffer unnecessarily and were raised in a way that didn't pollute the environment.

And for consumers who can't get to or don't have a farmers market in their area, Heritage Foods USA is shipping grass-fed, humanely-raised pigs, chickens, turkeys, and lambs to consumers all over the United States.[20] But these breeds of livestock aren't the ones we're accustomed to finding in large grocery stores. Many are rare and on the brink of extinction, and eating them is one of the only ways to save them. Consider the Red Wattle, a breed of pig originally introduced to North America in the 1700s. Named for its color and for the wattles of skin hanging beneath its chin, the Red Wattle may be the most at-risk livestock variety in the United States. During the eighteenth century, most producers raised pigs for their lard, but the red wattle has a very lean meat, which made it less desirable. It was practically extinct until a wild herd was discovered in Texas just a few decades ago. According to Patrick Martins, founder of Slow Food USA and co-founder of Heritage Foods USA, "while pandas and spotted owls will be saved in zoos and wildlife preserves, breeds like the Red Wattle and the Tunis lamb, whose job in life is to be food, will only be saved by being reintroduced onto American dinner tables."[21]

Keeping animals in zoos and embryos frozen in gene banks—known as ex-situ conservation—has been an effective, though costly, approach. But it is not very useful to people who depend on livestock agriculture for their livelihoods. A far more effective and productive way for farmers to preserve livestock breeds is on the farm, especially if farmers raise varieties with high monetary value. For example, the multicolored hides of N'guni cattle in South Africa are currently "en vogue" for furniture coverings. South African hut pigs are also becoming popular because of the large amount of fat they produce to make crackling, or fried pork skin, for the local market. These pigs sell for as much as 1,000 rand (US$150), much more than commercial pigs fetch.[22]

Beyond their market value or "trendiness," there are

other reasons to preserve diverse breeds of livestock. Conserving farm animal genetic diversity is a low-cost way of protecting food security in developing countries. According to Dr. Jacob Wanyama of the Intermediate Development Technology Group, "it is important to conserve not only animal genetic resources currently or likely to be used in the future for food and agriculture, but also ensure that the people who have conserved them for their livelihoods continue to do so."[23] For many of the world's poor living in arid and semiarid regions, livestock are the only efficient means of food production.

In October 2003, leaders of traditional pastoral communities, non-governmental groups, and government representatives met in Karen, Kenya, to draft the Karen Commitment. The document called for the protection of animal genetic resources from patenting and for greater recognition of pastoralists for their efforts to conserve and protect domestic animal breeds.[24]

Even some corporations are beginning to change their minds about how meat is made. In 2000, bowing to pressure from animal rights and public health groups, McDonald's announced that it would require producers to expand the space for hens in battery cages and that it would not buy from producers who force hens to lay additional eggs through starvation, practices already banned in Europe but still permitted in the United States.[25] McDonald's also now requires its suppliers to stop giving birds certain classes of antibiotics to promote growth, and gives preference to indirect suppliers who don't use these drugs over those who do.[26] Since McDonald's is one of the largest chicken buyers in the United States, the decision to change its standards will likely have a domino effect on the entire meat industry.

McDonald's, Wendy's, and Burger King have all recently hired specialists to research and devise new standards to improve animal welfare. In 1997, McDonald's hired renowned animal behavior specialist Temple Grandin to design slaughterhouses that are less stressful to livestock. Grandin is autistic and says this allows her to see, literally, what animals see. Based on this insight, she has designed entrances into slaugh-

COUNTRY STUDY 6

United States

Factory farms are not just moving to developing countries, but, ironically, to the United States as well. Western European nations now have some of the strongest environmental regulations for farms in the world. Producers in the Netherlands, for example, are only allowed to apply manure during certain times of the year and must follow strict controls on how much ammonia is released from their farms. As a result, a number of Dutch and German farmers are relocating to Ohio, Michigan, Wisconsin, and other states in the American Midwest. An Ohio-based company, Vebra-Hoff Dairy Development, is helping many of them make the move by identifying land for them to buy.

But the pollution and odor from these farms have upset nearby residents. In 2001, five Dutch-owned dairies were cited by the Ohio Environmental Protection Agency for manure spills, and all 44 Dutch-owned dairies in the U.S. have violated air and water pollution regulations. In 2005, residents of Greene County, Ohio, protested a permit for the construction of a new 2,000-head dairy operation, claiming the Dutch-proposed factory farm would contaminate local wells.

Such "takeovers" are likely to continue both in the U.S. and elsewhere. "Until there are international regulations controlling the waste from factory farms," says William Weida of the Global Reaction Center for the Environment/Spira Factory Farm project, "it is impossible to prevent farms from moving to places with less regulation."

Sources: See Endnote 6a, p. 85.

terhouses that have gradual inclines rather than steep ramps, as well as areas that give animals the opportunity to rest before slaughter.[27]

Two of the largest natural food chains in the United States are also ensuring that the animal products they sell are raised humanely. In 2005, Whole Foods Market, a Texas-based chain with over $3 billion in sales, committed more than $500,000 to establishing a foundation to study humane animal farming methods.[28] And both Whole Foods and Wild Oats, another U.S. natural food store chain, announced new policies in mid-2005 to sell only cage-free eggs at their stores.[29]

But don't think labels advertising "organic" or even "free-range" products necessarily mean that animals are treated well. Take Horizon Organics, for example. It is the largest producer of organic milk in the United States, with more than $255 million in annual sales.[30] But Horizon cows may not be as happy as they look on the package. Although the company doesn't use antibiotics, rBGH, or other hormones on its cows, its herds comprise thousands of animals, often crowded together in long barns. Essentially, say consumer groups, Horizon and another organic dairy producer, Colorado-based Aurora Dairy, are running organic factory farms. "People are paying more for organic products because they think the farmers are doing it right, that they're treating animals humanely and that the quality of the product is different," says Ronnie Cummins, national director of the Organic Consumers Association, a network of 600,000 organic consumers. "There has never been farms like Horizon or Aurora in the history of organics. Intensive confinement of animals is a no-no. This is Grade B organics."[31]

International policymaking and funding institutions are changing the way they think about livestock production as well. In 2001, the World Bank made a surprising reversal of its previous commitment to fund large-scale livestock projects in developing nations. In its new livestock strategy, the Bank acknowledged that as the sector grows, "there is a significant danger that the poor are being crowded out, the environment eroded, and global food safety and security threatened."[32] It has promised to use a "people-centered approach" to livestock development projects that will reduce poverty, protect environmental sustainability, ensure food security, and promote animal welfare.

This turnaround happened not because of pressure from activists, but because the large-scale, intensive animal production methods the World Bank once advocated are simply too costly. Past policies drove out smallholders because economies of scale for large units do not internalize the environmental costs of producing meat. The Bank's new strategy includes integrating livestock-environment interactions into environmental impact assessments, correcting regulatory distortions that favor large producers, and promoting and developing markets for organic products.[33] These measures are steps in the right direction, but more needs to be done by lending agencies, governments, non-governmental organizations, and individual consumers.

In another significant move, in June 2005 the 167 member countries of the World Organization for Animal Health (OIE) unanimously adopted standards for the humane transportation and slaughter of animals.[34] These include allowing animals adequate rest before slaughter and using improved stunning techniques. Although the standards are voluntary, they represent an important move towards legitimizing the humane treatment of farm animals worldwide.

And in July 2005, in an unprecedented decision, the U.S. Food and Drug Administration banned the use of Cipro-like antimicrobial drugs for poultry—including Baytril, manufactured by Bayer Corporation.[35] This marked the first time the U.S. government has pulled an agricultural antibiotic from the market because of concerns of antibiotic resistance affecting human health. While Bayer still claims that Baytril is necessary for poultry production, several large producers, including Tyson Foods, Inc., had already stopped using the drugs in their chickens.[36]

A month later, food service giant Compass Group North America partnered with pork producer Smithfield Foods and environmental group Environmental Defense to develop a first-of-its-kind purchasing policy to curb antibiotic use in pork production. The policy prohibits Compass's U.S. operations from buying pork from suppliers who use growth-promoting antibiotics that belong to classes of drugs important for human medicine. It also requires suppliers to report and reduce their antibiotic use.[37]

But changing the ways huge agribusiness corporations do business is a difficult challenge. For years, these companies have defended factory farming as the most efficient, cost-effective way to produce meat, especially as demand increases. Recent studies by the International Food Policy Research Institute in the Philippines, Brazil, and Thailand, however, suggest that small livestock farms may be more efficient at generating profits per unit of output than are large production operations, especially if farmers take steps to be involved in vertical coordination with processors and input suppliers.[38]

Some critics also say that improving farm-animal welfare is too expensive and could drive up the cost of food. But a recent report by Michael Appleby of the Humane Society of the United States finds that *not* implementing animal welfare standards on farms can result in diminishing returns for producers.[39] The article also notes that because the expense of housing and feeding animals represents only a small portion of the final cost to consumers, improving animal welfare would lead to only a small rise in retail prices. According to Appleby, "increasing the cost of production by 10 percent only need add 0.5 percent to the price of the meal. Most consumers would not even notice a change and it seems likely they would support it if asked."[40] Overall, consumer support for animal welfare issues appears to be growing: a 2003 Gallup poll found that 62 percent of Americans favor passing strict laws concerning the treatment of farm animals.[41]

Producers also claim that limiting antibiotic usage on their farms would be too costly, driving up production costs and retail prices for consumers. But a voluntary ban by Danish farmers on such drugs in the 1990s actually cut costs by dramatically decreasing the prevalence of resistant bacteria. Before the ban, 80 percent of Denmark's chickens carried vancomycin-resistant eneterococcus; today, only 10 percent do. Prevalence of resistant bacteria in pigs dropped from 65 percent to 25 percent. Through health monitoring programs, producers have also reduced the spread of salmonella from livestock to humans without resorting to antibiotics, saving the country $25.5 million in 2001.[42]

Furthermore, the true costs of animal production are not reflected in the price consumers currently pay at the store. Imagine, for example, if the price tags on chicken and turkey products included the costs of rising antibiotic resistance? Or if the bill at fast-food restaurants included the increasing health care costs from obesity, cardiovascular disease, and cancer?

Ultimately, we, as consumers, will have to reconsider

the place of meat in our diets. Reversing the human health and environmental problems caused by our appetite for modern meat will by necessity mean eating fewer animal products. Animals raised on pasture do not mature as quickly as feedlot animals do, and rangelands support fewer total animals than can be squeezed into feedlots.

But consumers have plenty of options, from adopting a vegan diet or adding a few vegetarian meals a week to supporting producers of local, organic, or pasture-raised livestock. The Center for a Livable Future at the Johns Hopkins School of Public Health encourages people to have a "Meatless Monday" and to try different plant-based menus.[43] The *Eat Well Guide* developed by the Institute for Agriculture and Trade Policy provides consumers in the United States with an easy way to find locally produced meat and other animal products.[44] And while the USDA's food pyramid still emphasizes diets high in animal-based protein (thanks to the influence of the meat and dairy lobbies), other countries are developing guidelines that educate consumers about the benefits of eating less meat.[45] The German food pyramid, for example, emphasizes lowering saturated-fat intake by eating fewer animal products.[46]

For governments, taking steps to ensure the safety of the meat and animal products we eat could be among the most important investments in homeland security. Since September 11, 2001, food security has taken on a new meaning. The sheer scale and economic importance of agriculture, particularly in industrial countries, make it an easy target for terrorist acts.[47] According to Peter Chalk, an agro-terrorism expert at the RAND Corporation, industrial farms are especially attractive targets.[48]

Not just the animals, but also the meat and dairy they produce, are vulnerable to attack. A June 2005 report in the *Proceedings of the National Academy of Sciences* notes that just a third of an ounce of botulism poured by bioterrorists into a dairy tanker truck could cause hundreds of thousands of deaths and billions of dollars in economic losses in the U.S. alone. Because the milk from multiple farms is consolidated in tankers, the toxin could be widely distributed and consumed within days by more than 500,000 people.[49]

But it's not just about keeping factory farms safe from disease outbreaks. It's about changing our whole view of what animal agriculture could look like. From a systems point of view, factory farming is similar to other large environmentally destructive enterprises, such as fossil fuel extraction or timber clearcutting. Subsidies for these practices, as for industrial agriculture, allow them to profit without accounting for their full environmental and public health costs. The real challenge, and the real reward, will come from approaching the way we raise food in a different way.

Changing the meat economy will require rethinking our relationship with livestock and the price we're willing to pay for safe, sustainable, and humanely-raised food. Meat is not just a dietary component, it's a symbol of wealth and prosperity. Reversing the factory-farm tide will require thinking about farming systems as more than a source of economic wealth. Preserving prosperous family farms and their landscapes and raising healthy and humanely-treated animals are their own form of affluence.

Endnotes

The Jungle, Revisited

1. Cees de Haan, Henning Steinfeld, and Harvey Blackburn, "Livestock and the Environment: Finding a Balance," a report of a study coordinated by the U.N. Food and Agriculture Organization (FAO), the United States Agency for International Development, and the World Bank (Brussels: European Commission Directorate-General for Development, 1997), p. 8.

2. FAO, FAOSTAT Statistical Database, at apps.fao.org, updated 20 December 2004.

3. European Commission, U.K. Department for International Development, and IUCN-The World Conservation Union, "Livestock and Biodiversity," Biodiversity Brief 10 (Brussels and Gland, Switzerland: Biodiversity in Development Project, undated), p. 1; Simon Anderson, "Animal Genetic Resources and Livelihoods," *Ecological Economics*, Special Issue on Animal Genetic Resources, July 2003, pp. 331–39.

4. FAO, "The Globalizing Livestock Sector: Impact of Changing Markets," Item 6 of the Provisional Agenda, 19th Session of the Committee on Agriculture, Rome, 12–16 April 2005, at www.fao.org/docrep/meeting/009/j4196e.htm.

5. de Haan et al., op. cit. note 1.

6. European Commission et al., op. cit. note 3.

7. Ibid.

8. Ibid.

9. Figure 1 from FAO, op. cit. note 2.

10. FAO, op. cit. note 2.

11. Figure 2 from FAO, op. cit. note 2.

12. Data and Figure 3 from FAO, op. cit. note 2.

13. Christopher L. Delgado and Claire A. Narrod, "Impact of Changing Market Forces and Policies on Structural Change in the Livestock Industries of Selected Fast-Growing Developing Countries, Final Research Report of Phase I—Project on Livestock Industrialization, Trade, and Social-Health-Environment Impacts in Developing Countries" (Rome: International Food Policy Research Institute (IFPRI) and FAO, 28 June 2002).

14. Christopher Delgado et al., "Livestock to 2020: The Next Food Revolution," *Food, Agriculture, and the Environment Discussion Paper 28* (Washington, DC:

IFPRI, FAO, and International Livestock Research Institute, May 1999).

15. Christopher Delgado, IFPRI, e-mails to author, March 2005.

16. Delgado and Narrod, op. cit. note 13.

17. Christopher Delgado, Mark Rosegrant, and Nikolas Wada, "Meating and Milking Global Demand: Stakes for Small-Scale Farmers in Developing Countries," in A.G. Brown, ed., *The Livestock Revolution: A Pathway from Poverty? A record of a conference conducted by the Australian Academy of Technological Sciences and Engineering Crawford Fund at Parliament House, Canberra, 13 August 2003* (Parkville, Victoria, Australia: The ATSE Crawford Fund, 2003).

18. Christopher L. Delgado, Claude B. Courbois, and Mark W. Rosegrant, "Global Food Demand and the Contribution of Livestock As We Enter the New Millennium," *MSSD Discussion Paper No. 21* (Washington, DC: IFPRI, February 1998), p. 6.

19. de Haan et al., op. cit. note 1, p. 53.

20. FAO, "Meat and Meat Products," *FAO Food Outlook No. 4*, October 2002, p. 11.

21. Upton Sinclair, *The Jungle* (New York: Doubleday, Page, & Company, 1906).

22. Mary Hendrickson and William Heffernan, "Concentration of Agricultural Markets" (Columbia, MO: University of Missouri Columbia, Department of Rural Sociology, February 2005).

23. Ibid.

24. Quote from Tyson Foods, Inc., "Company Information," at www.tyson foodsinc.com/corporate/info/today.asp, viewed 27 July 2005; Tyson Foods, Inc., *2004 Annual Report*, available at media.corporate-ir.net/media_files/irol/65/ 65476/reports/ar04.pdf.

25. Smithfield Foods, "Acquisitions at a Glance," at www.smithfieldfoods .com/Understand/Acquisitions, viewed 27 July 2005.

26. Public Citizen, "Smithfield Foods: A Corporate Profile: The Story Behind the World's Biggest Pork Producer" (Washington, DC: June 2004).

27. David A. Hennessy, John A. Miranowski, and Bruce A. Babcock, "Genetic Information in Agricultural Productivity in Product Development," Staff General Research Papers No. 10340 (Ames, IA: Iowa State University Center for Agricultural and Rural Development, April 2003); $0.62 from John Steele Gordon, "The Chicken Story," *American Heritage*, September 1996, pp. 52–67.

28. Ibid.

29. F.T. Jones and S.C. Ricke, "Observations on the History of the Development of Antimicrobials and their Use in Poultry Feeds," *Poultry Science*, vol. 82 (2003), pp. 613–17; David Wallinga, Institute for Agriculture and Trade Policy, e-mail to author, July 2005.

30. Stuart Laidlaw, *Secret Ingredients: The Brave New World of Industrial Farming* (Toronto: McClelland & Stewart, Ltd., 2003).

31. Ibid.

32. Hennessy et al., op. cit. note 27; Gordon, op. cit. note 27.

33. Estimate of 13 kilograms from Hennessy et al., op. cit. note 27; 22 kilograms from National Research Council, *The Use of Drugs in Food Animals, Benefits and Risks* (Washington, DC: National Academy Press, 1999), p. 29.

34. Mack O. North, *Commercial Chicken Production Manual, 3rd ed.* (Westport, CT: AVI Publishing Company, Inc., undated), p. 3.

35. Sidebar 1 based on the following sources: Ian Duncan, "Welfare Problems of Poultry," in G.J. Benson and B.E. Rollin, eds., *The Well-Being of Farm Animals* (Ames, IA: Blackwell Publishing, 2004), pp. 307–23; Laidlaw, op. cit. note 30, pp. 31, 52; United Egg Producers, *Animal Husbandry Guidelines for U.S. Egg Laying Flocks, 2003 Edition*, p. 13; J. Mench and J. Swanson, "Developing Science-Based Animal Welfare Guidelines," paper presented at Poultry Symposium and Egg Processing Workshop, 2000, available at animalscience.ucdavis.edu/Avian/mench.pdf; United States Department of Agriculture (USDA), National Agricultural Statistics Service, "Chickens and Eggs: 2004 Summary" (Washington, DC: February 2005), at usda.mannlib.cornell.edu/reports/nassr/poultry/pec-bbl/lyegan05.txt; Anthony Browne, "Ten Weeks to Live," *The Observer*, 10 March 2002; Gary Thornton and Terrence O'Keefe, "Housing and Equipment Survey," *WATT Poultry USA*, June 2001, pp. 38–47; feed amount from Richard Reynnells, National Program Leader, Animal Production Systems, USDA, e-mail to author, 26 September 2003, and from North, op. cit. note 34, p. 374; Consumers Union, "Presence of Anti-microbial Resistant Pathogens in Retail Poultry Products: A Report by CI Members in Australia and the United States," presented by Consumers International to the Codex Committee on Residues of Veterinary Drugs in Foods, 4–7 March 2003; John Webster, *Animal Welfare: A Cool Eye Towards Eden* (Oxford, UK: Blackwell Publishing, 1995), p. 128; "In Praise of Family Poultry," *Agriculture 21* (FAO), March 2002.

36. For more information on how animals are raised on factory farms, see USDA, Animal Plant and Health Inspection Service, at www.aphis.usda.gov; Grace Factory Farm Project, at www.factoryfarm.org; Humane Society of the United States, at www.hsus.org; and Animal Welfare Institute, at www.awionline.org.

37. USDA, "Volume 1 Chapter 1: U.S. National Level Data," *2002 Census of*

Agriculture, available at www.nass.usda.gov/census02/volume1/us/index1.htm.

The Disassembly Line

1. Human Rights Watch, *Blood, Sweat, and Fear, Workers' Rights in U.S. Meat and Poultry Plants* (New York: 2005), p. 11.

2. Ibid, pp. 12–13.

3. Eric Schlosser, *Fast Food Nation: The Dark Side of the All-American Meal* (New York: Houghton Mifflin Company, 2001).

4. "Southeast: North Carolina, Kentucky," *Rural Migration News* (University of California, Davis), January 1999, available at migration.ucdavis.edu/rmn/more.php?id=333_0_2_0.

5. Cecelia Ambos, health inspector, Tondo slaughterhouse, Manila, the Philippines, personal communication with author, August 2003.

6. Schlosser, op. cit. note 3.

7. U.S. Department of Agriculture (USDA), Animal Plant and Health Inspection Service, at www.aphis.usda.gov; Humane Society of the United States, at www.hsus.org.

8. Ibid.

9. Sidebar 2 based on the following sources: catch and harvest numbers from U.N. Food and Agriculture Organization (FAO), FAOSTAT Statistical Database, at apps.fao.org, updated 20 December 2004; projections from Christopher L. Delgado et al., "Outlook for Fish to 2020. Meeting Global Demand" (Washington, DC and Penang, Malaysia: International Food Policy Research Institute (IFPRI) and WorldFish Center, October 2003); fish meal, overharvesting, and disease from Rosamund Naylor et al., "Effect of Aquaculture on Global Fish Supplies," *Nature*, 29 June 2000, pp. 1017–24; Institute for Agriculture and Trade Policy, "Open Ocean Aquaculture," fact sheet (Washington, DC: August 2004); Ronald A. Hites et al., "Global Assessment of Organic Pollutants in Farmed Salmon," *Science*, 9 January 2004, pp. 226–29.

10. Bruce Friedrich, Director of Vegan Campaigns, People for the Ethical Treatment of Animals, e-mail to author, July 2005.

11. Ronald Randel, Regents Fellow and Senior TAES Faculty Fellow, Department of Animal Science, Texas A&M University, Agricultural Research and Extension Center, e-mail to Sara Loveland, Worldwatch Institute, June 2005.

Appetite for Destruction

1. Figure 4 derived from the following sources: feed from Vaclav Smil, Department of Geography, University of Manitoba, discussion with Brian Halweil, Worldwatch Institute, October 2002, and from Mark Ash, Economic Research Service, U.S. Department of Agriculture, e-mail to author, May 2005; water from Erik Millstone and Tim Lang, *The Penguin Atlas of Food: Who Eats What, Where, and Why* (London: Penguin Books, 2003), p. 35; additives from Margaret Mellon, Charles Benbrook, and Karen Lutz Benbrook, *Hogging It! Estimates of Antimicrobial Abuse in Livestock* (Washington, DC: Union of Concerned Scientists, 2001); fossil fuels from Millstone and Lang, op. cit. this note, pp. 35, 62; methane from Cees de Haan, Henning Steinfeld, and Harvey Blackburn, "Livestock and the Environment: Finding a Balance," a report of a study coordinated by the U.N. Food and Agriculture Organization (FAO), the United States Agency for International Development, and the World Bank (Brussels: European Commission Directorate-General for Development, 1997), p. 79; diseases from Neil Barnard, Andrew Nicholson, and Jo Lil Howard, "The Medical Costs Attributed to Meat Consumption," *Preventive Medicine*, November 1995.

2.   Ash, op. cit. note 1.

3.   Ibid.

4.   Michael Pollan, "The Life of a Steer," *New York Times*, 31 March 2002.

5.   Interview with Michael Pollan, in Russell Schloch, "The Food Detective," *California Monthly*, December 2004.

6.   Pollan, op. cit. note 4.

7.   Ibid.

8.   "Hay! What a Way to Fight E. coli," *Science News Online*, 19 September 1998, at www.sciencenews.org/pages/sn_arc98/9_19_98/food.htm.

9.   Rosamund Naylor et al., "Effect of Aquaculture on Global Fish Supplies," *Nature*, 29 June 2000, pp. 1017–24.

10. U.S. Food and Drug Administration (FDA), "FDA Prohibits Mammalian Protein in Sheep and Cattle Feed," FDA Talk Paper, 3 June 1997. For more information on the ruminant feed ban, see FDA Center for Veterinary Medicine Web site, at www.fda.gov/cvm.

11. European Commission, "Regulation (EC) No. 999/2001 of the European Parliament and of the Council of 22 May 2001: Laying Down Rules for Prevention, Control and Eradication of Certain Transmissible Spongiform Encephalopathies" (Brussels: 22 May 2001).

12. Sergio Gomez, Centro Nacional de Investigación de Fisiología Animal, Queretaro, México, personal communication with author, November 2004.

13. Millstone and Lang, op. cit. note 1, p. 35.

14. United Nations Commission on Sustainable Development, "Water—More Nutrition Per Drop, Towards Sustainable Food Production and Consumption Patterns in a Rapidly Changing World" (Stockholm: 2004).

15. Ibid.

16. Ibid.

17. United Nations Environment Programme, *Cleaner Production Assessment in Meat Processing* (Nairobi: October 2000), pp. v, 18.

18. Vivian Au, "ArchSD: Sheung Shui Slaughterhouse," Building Energy Efficiency Research Case Studies (Hong Kong: The University of Hong Kong Department of Architecture, undated), available at www.arch.hku.hk/teaching/cases/sheungsh/sheungsh.html#1.

19. Millstone and Lang, op. cit. note 1, p. 35.

20. Michael Mallin, "Impacts of Industrial Animal Agriculture on Rivers and Estuaries, *American Scientist*, January/February 2000.

21. Ibid.

22. Michael Mallin et al., "Impacts and Recovery from Multiple Hurricanes in a Piedmont-Coastal Plain River System," *Bioscience*, November 2002, p. 999.

23. Environmental Defense, "Hog Watch," at www.environmentaldefense.org/subissue.cfm?subissue=10, viewed 27 July 2005.

24. Danielle Nierenberg, "Toxic Fertility," *World Watch*, March/April 2001, p. 33.

25. Figure of 600 million from U.S. Environmental Protection Agency (EPA), "Concentrated Animal Feeding Operations (CAFO)—Final Rule, Chapter 1—Background Information," *Federal Register*, 12 February 2003, p. 7180, available at www.epa.gov/npdes/regulations/cafo_fedrgstr_chapt1.pdf; Alison Wiedeman, EPA, Office of Waste Water Management, Rural Branch, conversation with Sara Loveland, Worldwatch Institute, July 2005.

26. William J. Weida, "Concentrated Animal Feeding Operations and the Economics of Efficiency" (New York: GRACE Factory Farm Project, 19 March 2000).

27. Ibid.

28. Vaclav Smil, "Eating Meat: Evolution, Patterns, and Consequences," *Population and Development Review*, December 2002, p. 621.

29. U.S. Centers for Disease Control and Prevention, "Spontaneous Abortions Possibly Related to the Contamination of Nitrate-contaminated Well Water—

La Grange County Indiana, 1991–1994," *Morbidity and Mortality Weekly Report*, 5 July 1996.

30. M. Ward et al., "Drinking Water Nitrate and the Risk of Non-Hodgkin's Lymphoma," *Epidemiology*, September 1996, pp. 465–71.

31. Peter S. Goodman, "Chicken's Big Impact," *Washington Post*, 1 August 1999.

32. de Haan et al., op. cit. note 1, p. 55.

33. Steven R. Kirkhorn, "Community and Environmental Health Effects of Concentrated Animal Feeding Operations," *Minnesota Medicine*, October 2002.

34. Susan Schiffman et al., "The Effect of Environmental Odors Emanating from Commercial Swine Operations on the Mood of Nearby Residents," *Brain Research Bulletin*, vol. 37, no. 4 (1995), pp. 369–75; Kendall Thu et al., "A Control Study of the Physical and Mental Health of Residents Living Near a Large-Scale Swine Operation, *Journal of Agricultural Safety and Health*, vol. 3, no. 1 (1997), pp. 13–26; Amy Chapin, "Environmental Health Effects of Industrial Swine Production," speaker's kit (Poteau, OK: The Kerr Center for Sustainable Agriculture, undated).

35. Danielle Nierenberg, "Factory Farming in the Developing World," *World Watch*, May/June 2003, p. 14.

36. Pierre Gerber et al., "Geographical Determinants and Environmental Implications of Livestock Production Intensification in Asia," *Bioresource Technology*, vol. 96 (2005), pp. 263–76; Pierre Gerber, Livestock Environment Development Initiative, Livestock Information, Sector Analysis, and Policy Branch, FAO, discussion with author, April 2005.

37. "Canadian Town Wary of Water," *Associated Press*, 20 December 2000; "Waterborne Outbreak of Gastroenteritis Associated with Municipal Water Supply, Walkerton, Ontario, May-June 2000," *Canada Communicable Disease Report*, 15 October 2000.

38. J.C. Shanford, et al., "Occurrence and Diversity of Tetracycline Resistant Genes in Lagoons and Groundwater Underlying Two Swine Production Facilities," *Applied and Environmental Microbiology*, vol. 67, no. 4 (2001), pp. 1494–1502.

39. Edward Orlando et al., "Endocrine-Disrupting Effects of Cattle Feedlot Effluent on Aquatic Sentinel Species, the Fathead Minnow," *Environmental Health Perspectives*, 3 March 2004, p. 353.

40. Theo Colburn, Frederick vom Saal, and Ana Soto, "Developmental Effects of Endocrine Disrupting Chemicals on Wildlife and Humans," *Environmental Health Perspectives*, vol. 101 (1993), pp. 378–83.

41. United States District Court, Central District of Illinois, Springfield Division, "Test Drilling Service Co. v. Hanor Co., Inc., Pig Improvement Co., Inc., Agri-Waste Technology, Inc., Terracon, Inc., Barry Smith Enterprises, Inc., Lloyd Jones Construction, Envirotech Engineering & Consulting, Inc., Hog Slat, Inc.," No. 03-3063 (Springfield, IL: 24 June 2004).

Spreading Disease

1. United Nations Food and Agriculture Organization (FAO), "Loss of Domestic Animal Breeds Alarming," press release (Rome: 31 March 2004).

2. Ibid.

3. Ibid. Table 1 based on the following sources: cattle from "Environment Nepal: Indigenous Livestocks on Verge of Extinction," *Himalayan Times*, 1 December 2002; pig, chicken, and sheep from FAO, *World Watch List for Domestic Animal Diversity* (Rome: 2000), pp. 132, 517, 493; grouper from William K. Stevens, "Fierce Debate Erupts Over Degree of Peril Facing Ocean Species," *New York Times*, 17 September 1996.

4. Hope Shand, *Human Nature: Agricultural Biodiversity and Farm-based Food Security* (Pittsboro, NC: Rural Advancement Fund International, 1997).

5. Ibid.

6. Table 2 based on the following sources: World Health Organization (WHO), "Avian Influenza," fact sheet (Geneva: January 2004); FAO, Animal Health and Production Division, "Avian Influenza," Animal Health Special Report, at www.fao.org/ag/againfo/subjects/en/health/diseases-cards/special_avian.html; WHO, "Nipah Virus," fact sheet (Geneva: revised September 2001); WHO "Bovine Spongiform Encephalopathy," fact sheet (Geneva: revised November 2002).

7. Peter Chalk, RAND Corporation, personal communication with author, July 2004.

8. Peter Chalk, *Hitting America's Soft Underbelly: The Potential Threat of Deliberate Biological Attacks Against the U.S. Agricultural and Food Industry* (Arlington, VA: RAND Corporation, 2004).

9. Michael Specter, "Nature's Bioterrorist, Is There Any Way to Prevent a Deadly Avian-flu Pandemic?" *The New Yorker*, 28 February 2005.

10. WHO, "Avian Influenza," op. cit. note 6.

11. FAO, "High Geographic Concentration May Have Favored the Spread of Avian Flu," press release (Rome: 28 January 2004).

12. Alan Sipress, "As SE Asian Farms Boom, Stage Set for Pandemic," *Washington Post*, 5 February 2005.

13. Ibid.

14. Specter, op. cit. note 9.

15. Martin Enserink and Jocelyn Kaiser, "Avian Flu Finds New Mammal Hosts," *Science*, 3 September 2004, p. 1385.

16. Ibid.

17. FAO, FAOSTAT Statistical Database, at apps.fao.org, updated 20 December 2004.

18. Sipress, op. cit. note 12.

19. FAO, op. cit. note 6.

20. H. Chen et al., "The Evolution of H5N1 Influenza Viruses in Ducks in Southern China," *Proceedings of the National Academy of Sciences*, 13 July 2004, pp. 10452–57.

21. Dennis Normile, "Outbreak in Northern Vietnam Baffles Experts," *Science*, 22 April 2005, p. 477.

22. WHO, cited in ibid.

23. WHO, Communicable Disease Surveillance & Response, "Estimating the Impact of the Next Influenza Pandemic" (Geneva: 8 December 2004), at www.who.int/csr/disease/influenza/preparedness2004_12_08/en.

24. Declan Butler, "Vaccination Will Work Better Than Culling, Say Bird Flu Experts," *Nature*, 14 April 2005, p. 810.

25. FAO, "Enemy at the Gate: Saving Farms and People from Bird Flu," news release (Rome: 11 April 2005).

26. Butler, op. cit. note 24.

27. Ibid.

28. FAO, op. cit. note 17.

29. Emmanuelle Guerne-Bleich, Animal Production Officer, FAO, e-mail to author, 2004.

30. Center for Infectious Disease Research and Policy, "Vietnam to Expand Restrictions to Fight Avian Flu," CIDRAP News, 20 April 2005.

31. Ellen Nakashima, "Officials Urge Farm Overhauls to Avert Bird Flu Pandemic," *Washington Post*, 26 February 2005.

32. Paul Brown et al., "Bovine Spongiform Encephalopathy and Variant Creutzfeldt-Jacob Disease: Background, Evolution, and Current Concerns," *Emerging Infectious Diseases*, January-February 2001, pp. 6–14; WHO, "Bovine Spongiform Encephalopathy," op. cit. note 6.

33. WHO, "Bovine Spongiform Encephalopathy," op. cit. note 6.

34. Brown et al., op. cit. note 32.

35. Meat and bone meal from Erik Millstone and Tim Lang, *The Penguin Atlas of Food: Who Eats What, Where, and Why* (London: Penguin Books, 2003), p. 37.

36. John Gregerson, "Japan Ends Blanket Testing for Mad Cow Disease," meatingplace.com, 2 August 2005.

37. Mari Yamaguchi, "Japan Questioning Safety of U.S. Beef," *Associated Press*, 15 July 2005.

38. Brian Coffey et al., "The Economic Impact of BSE on the U.S. Beef Industry: Product Value Losses, Regulatory Costs, and Consumer Reactions" (Topeka, KS: Kansas State University, 2005); Peter Hisey, "K-State: BSE has Cost Industry Billions in Lost Exports," meating place.com, 29 April 2005.

39. Marc Kaufman, "U.S. Officials Confirm Second Mad Cow Case, *Washington Post*, 11 June 2005.

40. For more information, see the Consumers Union Web site, at www.consumersunion.org, and the Center for Media and Democracy Web site, at www.prwatch.org.

41. "Mad Cows May Have a New Form of BSE," *Agence France-Presse*, 18 February 2004.

42. John Tagliabue, "Mad Cow Disease Found in Goat," *New York Times*, 29 January 2005; "Suspected BSE Infection in Goat Confirmed," meatingplace.com, 31 January 2005.

43. Tagliabue, ibid.

44. Adriano Aguzzi et al., "Prions at Sites of Inflammation," *Science*, 18 February 2005, pp. 997–1152.

45. David Campbell, Professor Robert Lee, and Tamara Egede, "The UK Foot and Mouth Epidemic of 2001: A Research Resource" (Cardiff, UK: The ESRC Centre for Business Relationships, Accountability, Sustainability and Society, Cardiff University, updated 26 February 2004), at www.fmd.brass.cf.ac.uk.

46. Ibid.

47. Data for 1972 and 1996 from Government of the United Kingdom, Ministry of Agriculture, Fisheries and Food, *"The BSE Inquiry: The Report, Volume 13: Industry Processes and Controls* (London: October 2000), available at www.bseinquiry.gov.uk/report/volume13/chaptea2.htm; 2005 from U.K. Food Standards Agency, "Meat Premises Licensing," 21 July 2005, at www.food.gov.uk/foodindustry/meat/meatplantsprems/meatpremlicence.

48. Millstone and Lang, op. cit. note 35, p. 62.

49. Peter Fritsch, "Scientists Search for Human Hand Behind Outbreak of Jungle Virus," *Wall Street Journal*, 19 June 2003; Leslie Bienen, "Bats Suspected in Disease Outbreak," *Frontiers in Ecology*, April 2004, p. 117.

50. Ibid.

51. Peter Daszak, Executive Director, Consortium for Conservation Medicine, Wildlife Trust, e-mail to author, September 2004.

52. Wildlife Trust, "Nipah Virus Breaks Out in Bangladesh: Mortality Rates of 60 to 74 Percent, Human-to-Human Transmission May Be Implicated," press release (New York: 28 April 2004).

53. U.S. Centers for Disease Control and Prevention, "Update: Multi-state Outbreak of Eschericia coli 0157:H7 Infections from Hamburgers—Western United States, 1992–1993," *Morbidity and Mortality Weekly Report*, 16 April 1993.

54. J. Schlundt et al., "Emerging Food-borne Zoonoses," *Scientific and Technical Review*, August 2004. Table 3 based on the following sources: "Camplyobacter Jejun," in U.S. Food and Drug Administration and Center for Food Safety and Applied Nutrition, *Foodborne Pathogenic Microorganisms and Natural Toxins Handbook*, at vm.cfsan.fda.gov/~mow/intro.html, updated 8 March 2000; listeria from European Commission, Health & Consumer Protection Directorate-General, "Opinion of the Scientific Committee on Veterinary Measures Relating to Public Health on Food-Borne Zoonoses (Brussels: 12 April 2000), p. 22; parasites and *E. coli* from WHO, *Foodborne Disease: A Focus for Health Education* (Geneva: 2000); idem, "Multi-Drug Resistant Salmonella typhimurium," Fact Sheet No. 139 (Geneva: January 1997).

55. Ian Langford quoted in Nick Tattersall, "Stressed Farm Animals Contribute to Food Poisoning: U.K. Study," *Manitoba Co-Operator*, 15 March 2001.

56. Eric Schlosser, *Fast Food Nation: The Dark Side of the All-American Meal* (New York: Houghton Mifflin Company, 2001), p. 201.

57. Ibid., p. 203.

58. Paul Fey et al., "Ceftriaxone-Resistant Salmonella Infection Acquired by a Child from Cattle," *The New England Journal of Medicine*, 27 April 2000, pp. 1242–49.

59. Jay Varma et al., "Antimicrobial Resistant Nontyphoidal Salmonella is Associated With Excess Bloodstream Infections and Hospitalizations," *Journal of Infectious Disease*, 15 February 2005, pp. 554–61.

60. Meena Ramchandani et al., "Possible Animal Origin of Human-Associated, Multidrug-resistant Uropathogenic Escherichia Coli," *Clinical Infectious Diseases*, 15 January 2005, pp. 251–57.

61. Keep Antibiotics Working, "California Study Strengthens Link Between Antibiotic Overuse in Food Animals and Antibiotic-Resistant Urinary Tract Infections in Humans," press release (Washington, DC: 10 January 2005).

62. Margaret Mellon, Charles Benbrook, and Karen Lutz Benbrook, *Hogging It! Estimates of Antimicrobial Abuse in Livestock* (Washington, DC: Union of Concerned Scientists, 2001).

63. F.T. Jones and S.C. Ricke, "Observations on the History of the Development of Antimicrobials and their Use in Poultry Feeds," *Poultry Science*, vol. 82 (2003), pp. 613–17.

64. Mellon, Benbrook, and Benbrook, op. cit. note 62.

65. David Wallinga, Director, Food and Health Program, Institute for Agriculture and Trade Policy, discussion with author, June 2005.

66. Amy Chapin et al., "Airborne Multidrug-Resistant Bacteria Isolated from a Concentrated Swine Feeding Operation," *Environmental Health Perspectives*, February 2004, pp. 137–42.

67. Louise van der Merwe, "Scary Report Shows South Africa's Poor Are Being Dished Out Toxic Food," press release (Johannesburg: Compassion in World Farming South Africa, 2001).

68. R. Hanson et al., "Prevalence of Salmonella and E. coli and their Resistance to Antimicrobial Agents in Farming Communities in Northern Thailand," *Southeast Asian Journal of Tropical Medical Public Health*, Supplement 3 (2002), pp. 120–6; World Society for the Protection of Animals (WSPA), *Industrial Animal Agriculture—The Next Global Health Crisis?* (London: November 2004).

69. Legislation related to antibiotics ban available at European Union, "03.50.10 Animal Feedingstuffs," at europa.eu.int/eur-lex/lex/en/repert/035010.htm, viewed 29 July 2005.

70. WHO, "Use of Antimicrobial Drugs Outside Human Medicine and Resultant Antimicrobial Resistance in Humans," Fact Sheet No. 268 (Geneva: January 2002), available at www.who.int/mediacentre/factsheets/fs268/en/.

71. Gail Cassell and John Mekalanos, "Development of Antimicrobial Agents in the Era of New and Reemerging Infectious Diseases and Increasing Antibiotic Resistance," *Journal of the American Medical Association*, 7 February 2001, pp. 601–05.

72. Schlosser, op. cit. note 56.

73. Figures of 20 percent, two-thirds, and one-third from Lisa Archer, "Free Range, Not Factory Farmed, This is Your Beef on Drugs: The Health and Environmental Risks of Hormones in Meat," fact sheet (Washington, DC: Friends of the Earth, undated), at www.foe.org/factoryfarms/factsheet.html.

74. Ibid.; European Union, op. cit. note 69.

75. Archer, op. cit. note 73.

76. WSPA, op. cit. note 68.

77. Ronald A. Hites et al., "Global Assessment of Organic Pollutants in Farmed Salmon," *Science*, 9 January 2004, pp. 226–29.

78. L. Cordain et al., "Fatty Acid Analysis of Wild Ruminant Tissues: Evolutionary Implications for Reducing Diet-Related Chronic Disease," *European Journal of Clinical Nutrition*, March 2002, pp. 181–91.

79. Eat Wild, "Health Benefits of Grass-Fed Products," at www.eatwild.com/nutrition.html, viewed 29 July 2005.

80. Ibid.; Jo Robinson, *Why Grassfed is Best! The Surprising Benefits of Grassfed Meat, Eggs, and Dairy Products* (Vashon, WA: Vashon Island Press, 2000).

81. Ibid.

82. Cheryl Long and Lynn Keiley, "Is Agribusiness Making Food Less Nutritious?," *Mother Earth News*, June/July 2004.

83. Robinson, op. cit. note 80.

84. Ann Chao et al., "Meat Consumption and Risk of Colorectal Cancer," *Journal of the American Medical Association*, 12 January 2005, pp. 172–182.

85. Eunyoung Cho et al., "Premenopausal Fat Intake and Risk of Breast Cancer," *Journal of the National Cancer Institute*, vol. 95, no. 14 (2003), pp. 1079–85.

86. Barry Popkin, Professor of Nutrition, University of North Carolina School of Public Health, e-mail to Sara Loveland Worldwatch Institute, June 2005.

87. Ibid.

88. WHO, Global Strategy on Diet, Physical Activity and Health, "Obesity and Overweight," at www.who.int/dietphysicalactivity/publications/facts/obesity/en/index.html.

89. Sally Squire, "To Cut Fat, Eat Less Meat," *Washington Post*, 21 June 2005.

90. Millstone and Lang, op. cit. note 35.

91. Bruce Schreiner, "China Licking Its Fingers," *Associated Press*, 15 January 2005.

92. Saritha Rai, "Taste of India in U.S. Wrappers," *New York Times*, 29 April 2003.

Happier Meals

1. Treena Hein, "Gene Splicing Improves Pork Farm Waste," *New Agriculturalist*, 1 March 2005.

2. Roxanne Khamsi, "Transgenic Cows Have Udder Success," news@nature.com, 3 April 2005; Robert Wall et al., "Genetically Enhanced Cows Resist Intramammary Staphylococcus aureus Infection," *Nature Biotech*, 1 April 2005, pp. 445–51.

3. Michael Pollan, "An Animal's Place," *New York Times Magazine*, 4 January 2003.

4. Brian Halweil and Danielle Nierenberg, "Watching What We Eat," in Worldwatch Institute, *State of the World 2004* (New York: W.W. Norton and Company, 2004), pp. 68–85.

5. Ibid.

6. Danielle Nierenberg, "Factory Farming in the Developing World," *World Watch*, May/June 2003, p. 17.

7. Ibid.

8. Ibid.; Bobby Inocencio, Teresa Farms, Philippines, personal communication with author, August 2002; Teresa Farms, *Management Guide SASSO Free-Range Colored Chickens* (Rizal, Philippines: undated).

9. Nierenberg, op. cit. note 6.

10. Ibid.

11. Kim Severson, "Give 'em a Chance, Steers Will Eat Grass," *New York Times*, 1 June 2005.

12. Ibid.

13. Ibid.

14. Polyface Farms Web site, at www.polyface.com.

15. Jo Robinson, *Why Grassfed is Best! The Surprising Benefits of Grassfed Meat, Eggs, and Dairy Products* (Vashon, WA: Vashon Island Press, 2000).

16. Sidebar 3 is based on the following sources: beef exports and deforestation from David Kaimowitz et al., "Hamburger Connection Fuels Amazon Destruction, Cattle Ranching and Deforestation in Brazil's Amazon," Center for International Forestry Research (CIFOR) (Bogor, Indonesia: April 2004); Kaimowitz cited in CIFOR, "World Appetite for Beef Making Mincemeat Out of Brazilian Rainforest According to Report from Major International Forest Research Center," press release (Bogor, Indonesia: April 2004); Latin and South America from U.N. Food and Agriculture Organization (FAO), "Cattle Ranching is Encroaching on Forests in Latin America," press release (Rome: 8 June 2005); soybeans from Kristal Arnold, "Globalization: It's a Small World After All," *Food Systems Insider*, 1 May 2005; Fundo Brasileiro para a Biodiversidade (FUNBIO), "PAPs: Organic Meat Production in Patanal," at www.funbio.org.br/publique/web/cgi/cgilua.exe/sys/start.htm?UserActiveTemplate=funbio_english&infoid=171&sid=44, viewed 29 July 2005; Conservation International, "Green Cows," at investigate.conservation.org/xp/IB/expeditions/pantanal/day5/day5_issues.xml, viewed 29 July 2005.

17. Lois Caliri, "The Beef of Small Meat Processors," *Roanoke Times and World News*, 1 May 2005.

18. Heifer International, "Opening the Processing Bottleneck," meeting notes from 22 March 2005 obtained from Terry Wollen, Director of Animal Well-Being, Heifer International, e-mail to author, June 2005.

19. Penny Price Fee, Sustainable Foods for Siouxland, personal communication with author, April 2005.

20. Heritage Foods USA Web site, at www.heritagefoods.com.

21. Patrick Martins, co-founder, Heritage Foods USA, personal communication with author, June 2005.

22. Susie Emmett, "Conserving Animal Genetic Resources—The Race is On," *New Agriculturalist*, May 2004.

23. Jacob Wanyama, Intermediate Technology Development Group, e-mail to author, 10 April 2004.

24. "Karen Commitment: Pastoralist/Indigenous Livestock Keepers' Rights," Indigenous Livestock Breeders Workshop, Karen, Kenya, 27–30 October 2003, available at www.ukabc.org/karen.htm.

25. David Barboza, "Animal Welfare's Unexpected Allies," *New York Times*, 25 June 2003.

26. David Barboza with Sherri Day, "McDonald's Seeking Cut in Antibiotics in Its Meat," *New York Times*, 20 June 2003; "Fast Food, Not Fast Antibiotics," *New York Times*, 22 June 2003.

27. McDonald's Corporation Web site, at www.mcdonalds.com.

28. Annual sales from Whole Foods Market, Inc., *2004 Annual Report* (Austin, TX: 2005); Whole Foods Market, Inc. "Whole Foods Market to Donate More than $550,000 to Seed Creation of Animal Compassion Foundation," press release (Austin, TX: 26 January 2005).

29. Humane Society of the United States, "Wild Oats and Slow Food Sow Compassion with Cage Free Policy," press release (Washington, DC: 3 June 2005).

30. Barbara Murray, "Horizon Organic Holding Corporation," research available on Hoovers, Inc., www.hoovers.com, 29 July 2005.

31. Cummins quoted in Rebecca Clarren, "Land of Milk and Honey," Salon.com, 13 April 2005.

32. Cornelius de Haan et al., *Directions in Development, Livestock Development, Implications for Rural Poverty, the Environment, and Global Food Security* (Washington, DC: World Bank, November 2001), pp. xii–xiii.

33. Ibid.

34. World Organization for Animal Health, "Guidelines for the Slaughter of Animals for Human Consumption," at www.oie.int/downld/SC/2005/animal_welfare_2005.pdf.

35. U.S. Food and Drug Administration (FDA), Department of Health and Human Services, "Final Decision of the Commissioner, Docket No. 2000N-1571, Withdrawal of Approval of the New Animal Drug Application for Enrofloxacin in Poultry," available at www.fda.gov/oc/antimicrobial/baytril.pdf.

36. "Narrative Statement of Respondent Bayer Corporation Pursuant to 21 CFR § 12.85 On the Proposal to Withdraw Enrofloxacin (NADA 140828) for Use in Poultry," FDA Hearing, Bayer Submissions, 1 May 2002; Marian Burros, "Poultry Industry Quietly Cuts Back on Antibiotic Use," *New York Times*, 10 February 2002, p. 1.

37. Environmental Defense, "Innovative Partnership First to Reduce Antibiotics Use in Mainstream Pork Production," press release (New York: 2 August 2005).

38. Christopher Delgado et al., "Meating and Milking Demand: Stakes for Small-Scale Farmers in Developing Countries" (Washington, DC: International Food Policy Research Institute, May 2004).

39. Michael Appebly, "The Relationship Between Food Prices and Animal Welfare," *Journal of Animal Science*, June 2005, pp. E9–E12.

40. Ibid.

41. David Moore, "Public Lukewarm on Animal Rights" (Princeton, NJ: The Gallup Organization: 21 May 2003), at www.gallup.com/poll/content/login.aspx?ci=8461.

42. Henrik C. Wegener et al., "*Salmonella* Control Programs in Denmark," *Emerging Infectious Diseases*, July 2003.

43. Meatless Monday Web site, at www.meatlessmonday.com.

44. Institute for Agriculture and Trade Policy, Eat Well Guide Web site, at www.eatwellguide.org.

45. U.S. Department of Agriculture, Center for Nutrition Policy and Promotion, MyPyramid.gov Web site, at www.mypyramid.gov, viewed 29 July 2005.

46. Astrid Potz, Department of Nutrition, German Agriculture Ministry, e-mail to author, April 2005.

47. Peter Chalk, RAND Corporation, personal communication with author, July 2004; idem, *Hitting America's Soft Underbelly: The Potential Threat of Deliberate Biological Attacks Against the U.S. Agricultural and Food Industry* (Arlington, VA: RAND Corporation, 2004).

48. Ibid.

49. Lawrence Wein and Yifan Liu, "Analyzing a Bioterror Attack on the Food Supply: The Case of Botulinum Toxin in Milk," *Proceedings of the National Academy of Sciences*, June 2005, pp. 9984–89.

Country Studies

1a. Poland study based on the following: Tom Hundley, "Village in Poland Clashes with U.S. Pork Giant; America's Top Hog Producer Wants to Create the Iowa of Europe; Residents Gag on Transformation," *Chicago Tribune*, 7 February 2005; Tom Garret, "Polish Delegation Investigates American Agribusiness, Repudiates Factory Farming," *AWI Quarterly* (Animal Welfare Institute), fall/winter 1999-2000.

2a. Mexico study based on the following: Eugenio Salinas Morales, Consejo Mexicano de la Carne, México City, México, personal communication with author, November 2004; Sergio Gomez, Centro Nacional de Investigación en Fisilogía Animal, Querétero, México, personal communication with author, November 2004.

3a. China study based on the following: Christopher Delgado et al., "Meating and Milking Demand: Stakes for Small-Scale Farmers in Developing Countries" (Washington, DC: International Food Policy Research Institute (IFPRI), May 2004); David Brubaker, agribusiness consultant, e-mail to author, May

2005; meat consumption from Delgado, op. cit. this note; CAFOs from The China-US Agro-Environmental Center of Excellence, informational brochure (Beijing, China: 2003); manure from Betsy Tao, "A Stitch in Time: Addressing the Environmental, Health, and Animal Welfare Effects of China's Expanding Meat Industry," *Georgetown International Law Review*, vol. 321 (2003), pp. 321–57.

4a. India study based on the following: milk production and broiler numbers from U.N. Food and Agriculture Organization (FAO), FAOSTAT Statistical Database, apps.fao.org, updated 20 December 2004; Operation Flood from Christopher Delgado and Claire Narrod, *Impact of Changing Market Forces and Policies on Structural Change in the Livestock Industries of Selected Fast-Growing Developing Countries, Final Research Report of Phase I—Project on Livestock Industrialization, Trade, and Social-Health-Environment Impacts in Developing Countries* (Rome: IFPRI and FAO, 2002).

5a. Brazil study based on the following: Kristal Arnold, "Globalization: It's a Small World After All," *Food Systems Insider*, 1 May 2005; Andrew Martin, "US Venture Hints at Brazil's Hog Farm Potential," *Chicago Tribune*, 14 June 2004; "Chile Cuts Emissions, Helps Japan, Canada. Chile Reducing Methane Fumes from Animal Waste, Trading Global Warming Credits to Japan, Canada," *Associated Press*, 3 January 2005.

6a. U.S. study based on the following: James Dao, "In Ohio, One Farmer's Prosperity is Another's Poison," *New York Times*, 26 March 2005; Amelia Robinson, "Dairy's Lawsuit Claims Zoning Regulation Illegal, *Dayton Daily News*, 22 July 2005; William Weida, GRACE Factory Farm project, personal communication with author, 2003.

Index

Other Worldwatch Papers

On Climate Change, Energy, and Materials
169: Mainstreaming Renewable Energy in the 21st Century, 2004
160: Reading the Weathervane: Climate Policy From Rio to Johannesburg, 2002
157: Hydrogen Futures: Toward a Sustainable Energy System, 2001
151: Micropower: The Next Electrical Era, 2000
149: Paper Cuts: Recovering the Paper Landscape, 1999
144: Mind Over Matter: Recasting the Role of Materials in Our Lives, 1998
138: Rising Sun, Gathering Winds: Policies To Stabilize the Climate and Strengthen Economies, 1997

On Ecological and Human Health
165: Winged Messengers: The Decline of Birds, 2003
153: Why Poison Ourselves: A Precautionary Approach to Synthetic Chemicals, 2000
148: Nature's Cornucopia: Our Stakes in Plant Diversity, 1999
145: Safeguarding the Health of Oceans, 1999
142: Rocking the Boat: Conserving Fisheries and Protecting Jobs, 1998
141: Losing Strands in the Web of Life: Vertebrate Declines and the Conservation of Biological Diversity, 1998
140: Taking a Stand: Cultivating a New Relationship With the World's Forests, 1998

On Economics, Institutions, and Security
168: Venture Capitalism for a Tropical Forest: Cocoa in the Mata Atlântica, 2003
167: Sustainable Development for the Second World: Ukraine and the Nations in Transition, 2003
166: Purchasing Power: Harnessing Institutional Procurement for People and the Planet, 2003
164: Invoking the Spirit: Religion and Spirituality in the Quest for a Sustainable World, 2002
162: The Anatomy of Resource Wars, 2002
159: Traveling Light: New Paths for International Tourism, 2001
158: Unnatural Disasters, 2001

On Food, Water, Population, and Urbanization
171: Happer Meals: Rethinking the Global Meat Industry, 2005
170: Liquid Assets: The Critical Need to Safeguard Freshwater Ecosytems, 2005
163: Home Grown: The Case for Local Food in a Global Market, 2002
161: Correcting Gender Myopia: Gender Equity, Women's Welfare, and the Environment, 2002
156: City Limits: Putting the Brakes on Sprawl, 2001
154: Deep Trouble: The Hidden Threat of Groundwater Pollution, 2000
150: Underfed and Overfed: The Global Epidemic of Malnutrition, 2000
147: Reinventing Cities for People and the Planet, 1999

Other Publications from the Worldwatch Institute

State of the World 2005
Worldwatch's flagship annual is used by government officials, corporate planners, journalists, development specialists, professors, students, and concerned citizens in over 120 countries. Published in more than 20 different languages, it is one of the most widely used resources for analysis. The authors of *State of the World 2005* propose that the foundations for peace and stability lie in moving away from dependence on oil, managing water conflicts, containing infectious diseases, moving toward disarmament, cultivating food security, and cooperating across borders to achieve a sustainable world.

Vital Signs 2005
Tracks major social, economic, and environmental indicators of our times.

> "*Vital Signs* provides the most straightforward and reliable environmental, economic, and social information available on the planet Earth. The book delivers…facts illuminated by contexts and interconnections, often revealing causes of the problems, and pointing the way towards solutions that work."
> —*Publishers Weekly*

State of the World Library 2005
Subscribe to the State of the World Library and join thousands of decisionmakers and concerned citizens who stay current on emerging environmental issues. For 2005 the Library includes our flagship annual *State of the World 2005: Redefining Global Security*, *Vital Signs 2005*, *Inspiring Progress: Religions' Contributions to Sustainable Development*, and Worldwatch Papers *Liquid Assets: The Critical Need to Safeguard Freshwater Ecosystems*, and *Happier Meals: Rethinking the Global Meat Industry*.

World Watch
This award-winning bimonthly magazine is internationally recognized for the clarity and comprehensiveness of its articles on global trends. Keep up-to-speed on the latest developments in population growth, climate change, species extinction, and the rise of new forms of human behavior and governance.

To make a tax-deductible contribution or to order any of Worldwatch's publications, call us toll-free at 888-544-2303 (or 570-320-2076 outside the U.S.), fax us at 570-320-2079, e-mail us at wwpub@worldwatch.org, or visit our website at www.worldwatch.org.

WORLDWATCH GLOBAL TRENDS

...economic, environmental, and social indicators for your research and presentation needs.

▶▶ Need reliable data on deaths from urban air pollution to help galvanize support for greater use of public transport?

▶▶ Ever wonder where you could find a chart or graph showing reliable comparisons of nitrogen fertilizer consumption around the globe?

▶▶ Would PowerPoint slides of economic and insured losses from weather-related disasters over time help you clinch a deal or underscore a point to your Board?

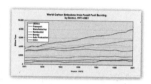

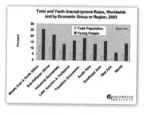

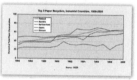

You can find these, and much more, in Worldwatch Institute's newest compilation of critical global trends covering economic, environmental, and social indicators—formerly known as Signposts—and now available as WORLDWATCH GLOBAL TRENDS.

This year's set of trends includes 184 updated indicators and 36 new ones, including new indicators for water in the Agriculture, Food, and Water Category; solar and biodiesel in the Energy category; and a brand new Ecosystems and Biodiversity category.

Each indicator is represented by charts, graphs, an Excel spreadsheet for manipulating the raw data, and PowerPoint slides for use in classroom and board-room presentations.

The nine categories of indicators are:

▶▶ AGRICULTURE, FOOD, AND WATER

▶▶ CLIMATE AND POLLUTION

▶▶ ECOSYSTEMS AND BIODIVERSITY

▶▶ CONFLICT AND PEACE

▶▶ ECONOMY

▶▶ ENERGY

▶▶ MATERIALS

▶▶ POPULATION AND HEALTH

▶▶ TRANSPORTATION AND COMMUNICATIONS

▶▶ Each of the 220 indicators is now available for purchase and download on Worldwatch's website at: www.worldwatch.org/pubs/globaltrends/ at the low price of $1.00 per indicator.

▶▶ For those who prefer to have a complete set of all 220 trends on a CD, prices are:
Nonprofits: $125
Corporations: $225

To order the CD:

▶▶ Call toll-free:
1.888.544.2303 or
570.320.2076

▶▶ Fax: 570.320.2079

▶▶ E-mail:
wwpub@worldwatch.org

www.worldwatch.org/pubs/globaltrends

Happier Meals
RETHINKING THE GLOBAL MEAT INDUSTRY

As livestock numbers grow, our relationship with these animals and their meat is changing. Most of us don't know—or choose not to know—how meat is made. But meat production has come a long way since the origins of animal domestication. In a very short period, raising livestock has morphed into an industrial endeavor that bears little relation to the landscape or to the natural tendencies of the animals.

Global meat production has increased five-fold since 1950, and industrial animal agriculture, or factory farming, is the fastest growing method of meat production worldwide. While livestock are an important source of income and nutrition for millions of people, the spread of factory farming in both industrialized and developing countries can have disastrous effects. From transmission of disease and loss of livestock diversity to hazardous and unsanitary processing methods, factory farming is an unsafe, inhumane, and ecologically disruptive form of meat production.

By supporting local, organic, or pasture-raised animal products, embracing alternative production methods, or adding a few vegetarian or vegan meals a week, farmers, processors, and consumers can help ensure that meat is made better for people, the environment, and the animals themselves.

WORLDWATCH
INSTITUTE

1776 Massachusetts Avenue, NW
Washington, DC 20036

09-AGB-145